To Karen ~
Happy Belated Birthday

Love Anthony xxx.

CRABTREE & EVELYN COOKBOOK

The CRABTREE & EVELYN COOKBOOK

☙

PHOTOGRAPHS BY
CHRISTOPHER BAKER

☙

BARRIE & JENKINS
LONDON

First published in Great Britain in 1989 by
Barrie & Jenkins Ltd
289 Westbourne Grove, London W11 2QA

British Library Cataloguing in Publication Data
The Crabtree & Evelyn cookbook.
1. Food: English dishes.—Recipes
I. Crabtree & Evelyn
641.5942
ISBN 0 7126 2082 6

NOTES
1. Measurements are given in both Metric and Imperial. As the
two are not exactly equivalent, follow only one set of measures
when preparing a recipe.
2. Spoon measures used are metric spoons (1 tablespoon =
15 ml and 1 teaspoon = 5 ml) and all are level.

Edited by Elizabeth Kent
Designed by Peter Windett

Printed in Japan

The illustrations reproduced on the following pages were
selected from copyrighted Crabtree & Evelyn packaging from
the years 1973–1988. Reproduction is by permission of the
copyright owner, Crabtree & Evelyn, Ltd. We are grateful for
the help and enthusiasm we have had from all the artists and
we would especially like to thank:

John Astrop
Ian Beck
Glynn Boyd-Harte
Braldt Bralds
Peter Brookes
Malcolm Chandler
Peter Church
Alan Cracknell
Fiona Bell Currie
Andrew Davidson
Brigid Edwards
Pauline Ellison
Graham Evernden
Hargrave Hands
Matthew Hillier
Ronald Lampitt
Carol Lawson
The Royal Horticultural Society (Lindley Library)
Jannat Messenger
Tony Meeuwissen
Karen Murray
Moira McGregor
Andrew McNab
Graham Percy
Marta Sietz
Richard Shirley-Smith
Povl Webb
Sue Windett

Recipe development: Brooke Dojny
   and Melanie Barnard
Recipe consultant: Mimi Errington
Assistant recipe consultant: Anne Higham
Prop stylist: Rebecca Gilles
Food stylist: Nigel Slater
Assistant food stylist: Adrian Barling

Prop credits:

All modern china, glass, and silver courtesy Chinacraft,
556 Oxford Street, Marble Arch, London W1N 9HJ

Rose punch bowl courtesy Asprey, 165-169 New Bond Street,
London W1Y 0AR

A well-stocked larder is an essential requirement for today's cooking. While undeniably, good quality, fresh ingredients are of the utmost importance, a secondary and equally interesting role is played by preserved foods. Jams, jellies, conserves, marmalades, honeys, oils, vinegars, herbs and spices fall into this category: They all contain fine seasonal ingredients which, in one way or another, are cooked or blended, then preserved, usually by sealing in glass jars.

For centuries, cooks have known the virtue of judicious seasoning—balancing sweet tastes with savoury, bringing out the flavour of meats and fish with complementary herbs, and using oils and vinegars to add character to salads and vegetable dishes. On the following pages we show how seemingly ordinary ingredients can subtly or, in some cases, dramatically, improve the taste of a recipe. Cornish Hens with Honey and Ginger, Cranberry-Port Sauce and Orange Flower Layer Cake are just a few examples.

In 1699, John Evelyn provided classic advice on the preparation of 'sallet dressing' in *Acetaria*: 'that the Oyl . . . be smooth, light and pleasant upon the tongue, that the Vinegar be of the best wine vinegar, that the salt be decisive, penetrating, quickening . . . that the mustard (another noble ingredient) be of the best Tewkesberry . . . that the pepper (white or black) be not bruised to too small a dust which, as we cautioned, is very prejudicial.' We hope that the recipes in this book will stand such a good test of time.

CRABTREE & EVELYN

TEA

DINNER

COCKTAILS

SUPPER

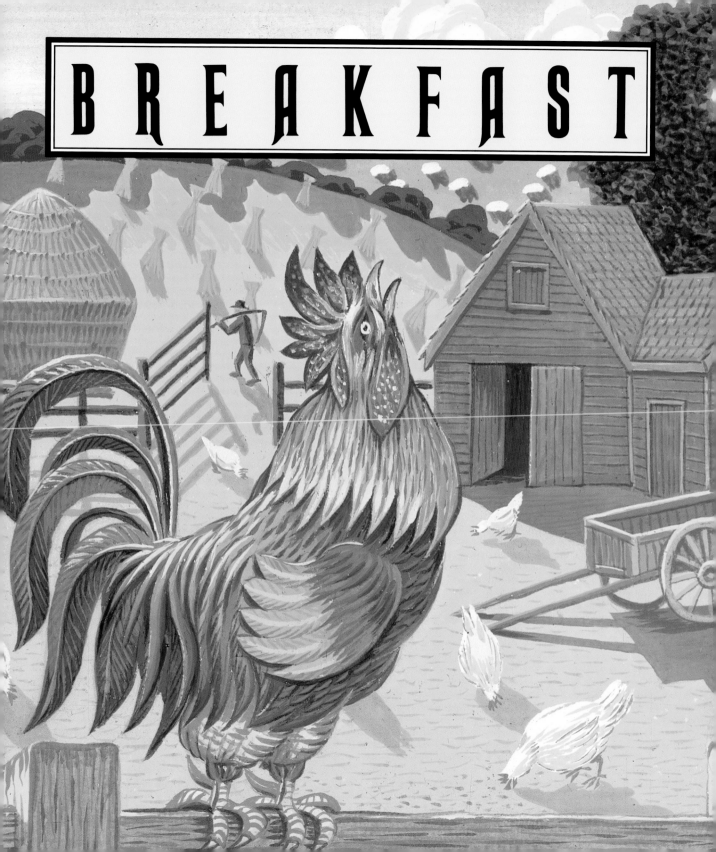

BREAKFAST

HERBAL EXTRACTS

MENU

◆

*S*AUTÉED TOMATO
CUBES

◆

*S*OFT-BOILED EGGS
WITH HERBS

◆

*B*RIOCHE JAM TOAST

OPPOSITE: BRIOCHE JAM TOAST,
SOFT-BOILED EGG WITH HERBS, AND
SAUTÉED TOMATO CUBES

To skin a tomato simply and quickly, spear the stalk end with a fork and dip it into a saucepan of boiling water for several seconds.

   Lift it out of the water, slit the skin with a small knife, and peel it off neatly. Remove the seeds by halving the tomato and scooping out the seed cavity with your fingers or a small spoon.

Sautéed Tomato Cubes

45   g/1½ oz butter
2   to 3 large ripe tomatoes (about 1 kg/2 lb), skinned, seeded, and cut into cubes
   Pinch sugar
   Salt
   Freshly ground pepper

In a large frying pan, melt butter, add tomatoes and sauté over high heat for 2 minutes, or until they are hot and their juices start to run. Sprinkle with sugar. Season with salt and pepper. Serve warm.

— 4 SERVINGS —

Soft-Boiled Eggs with Herbs

WHEN SELECTING EGGS TO BE SOFT-BOILED AND PEELED, CHOOSE ones that are several days old. With newly laid eggs, chunks of the white often come away with the shell as they are peeled. In addition to the herbs, freshly ground green peppercorns also look attractive.

The flowers of kitchen herbs and other edible blooms make delicate decorations for dishes throughout the meal.

   Bright nasturtium or soft chive blossoms on green salads, meat or fish; white basil flowers on sliced tomatoes; and tiny sprigs of rosemary with their mauve flowers on lemon soufflés—all hint at the possibilities of striking combinations.

4   size 3 eggs
   Salt
   Freshly ground pepper
10   to 12 sprigs fresh oregano, thyme, sage, rosemary or chervil, with blossoms if possible, leaves pulled from stalks

Bring a large saucepan of water to the boil over high heat. Gently lower eggs into the saucepan and allow water to return to a simmer. Reduce heat to medium and simmer gently for 3 minutes, stirring eggs carefully 2 to 3 times to centre their yolks. Using a slotted spoon, remove eggs from pan and rinse under tepid water to cool them slightly.

   Using the back of a spoon, gently crack the shell of each egg all over. Carefully peel away shells and place warm eggs in 4 separate serving bowls. Season eggs with salt and pepper and sprinkle each with fresh herbs and blossoms.

— 4 SERVINGS —

*B*RIOCHE JAM TOAST

THE BRIOCHE CAN EASILY BE MADE THE DAY BEFORE IT IS NEEDED, OR well in advance and frozen. Cooking jam toast on a ridged griddle creates an attractive pattern, especially if the slices of bread are placed diagonally. The toast can also be made simply by buttering and grilling single slices of brioche and then spreading them with jam.

8   5 mm/¼ inch thick slices brioche (see page 244),
     cut from centre of loaf
125 g/4 oz raspberry, blackcurrant or other berry jam
30   g/1 oz butter, softened

Spread 4 brioche slices with jam almost to the edges. Top each slice with 1 of the remaining 4 slices. Lightly butter both sides of each sandwich.

Preheat a ridged or flat griddle or frying pan until hot. Place sandwiches diagonally on the griddle and cook for 2 to 3 minutes per side, or until golden brown and crisp. Remove sandwiches from the griddle. Cut each sandwich into 4 equal strips and serve warm.

— 16 JAM TOASTS (4 TO 6 SERVINGS) —

Leftover brioche makes an exalted bread pudding. Sprinkle a few raisins and pieces of chopped citron between each layer of sliced brioche, pour the custard mixture over the top, and bake as indicated. As the pudding emerges from the oven, sprinkle it with a few teaspoons of cinnamon and sugar. Serve warm with cream.

STRAWBERRY
E X T R A   J A M
PRESERVE

Cooked slowly in open kettles and filled by hand.

PREPARED WITH
52 g OF FRUIT
PER 100 g
TOTAL SUGAR
CONTENT
66 g PER 100 g
INGREDIENTS: SUGAR,
STRAWBERRIES,
REDCURRANT JUICE.
© 1978. CRABTREE & EVELYN LTD.
WOODSTOCK HILL, CT 06281, USA.

Cuite lentement dans des chaudrons ouverts et mise en pots à la main.

PREPAREE AVEC
52 g DE FRUITS
POUR 100 g
TENEUR TOTALE
EN SUCRE
66 g POUR 100 g
INGREDIENTS: SUCRE,
FRAISES,
JUS DE GROSEILLES.
BOX 180, LONDON W8, UK.
FABRIQUE EN ANGLETERRE.

net wt 340 g 12 OZ

CONFITURE EXTRA
DE FRAISES
Crabtree & Evelyn®
L O N D O N
NO 5608. MADE IN ENGLAND. EMB 92036 S

poids 255 ml 9 oz fl

LAZY SUNDAY MORNING

MENU

◆

*T*ANGERINE-
GRAPEFRUIT JUICE

◆

*T*ARRAGON POACHED
EGGS

◆

*S*MOKED PORK LOIN
SAUTÉED IN BUTTER

◆

*O*AT WAFFLES

OPPOSITE: TANGERINE-GRAPEFRUIT
JUICE AND OAT WAFFLES

Tarragon's light but pervasive flavour particularly suits eggs, as well as mushrooms, carrots, mild fish, chicken and veal. It is the flavouring of the classic sauce béarnaise and enhances many salads when added—either chopped or included in the dressing via a tarragon vinegar or tarragon mustard.

Tangerine-Grapefruit Juice

6   tangerines (or clementines or satsumas), halved
3   medium grapefruit, halved

Using an electric or hand juicer, squeeze juice from tangerines and grapefruit. Combine the juices and chill.

— MAKES ABOUT 1 LITRE/1¾ PINTS —

Tarragon Poached Eggs

3   tablespoons tarragon vinegar
3   sprigs fresh tarragon, or ¼ teaspoon dried tarragon
4   size 3 eggs

TO SERVE
Fresh tarragon sprigs, chopped fresh tarragon or
dried tarragon (optional)

Fill a large frying pan with 750 ml/1¼ pints water, or enough to make a poaching bath at least 2.5 cm/1 inch deep. Add vinegar and tarragon. Bring this court bouillon to a simmer over medium-low heat.

Break each egg into a small cup, then carefully slide each into the court bouillon. Simmer gently for about 2 minutes, or until whites are set, spooning the hot liquid over eggs to lightly film yolks. Using a slotted spoon, remove eggs from liquid and sprinkle with fresh or dried tarragon, if desired. Serve warm.   — 4 SERVINGS —

Smoked Pork Loin
Sautéed in Butter

30   to 45 g/1 to 1½ oz unsalted butter
8   to 12 thin slices smoked pork loin or back bacon
     (175 to 250 g/6 to 8 oz)

In a large frying pan, melt butter over medium heat. Add pork and sauté until slices are heated through and are lightly browned, about 3 minutes. Do not overcook. Serve warm.   — 4 SERVINGS —

$\mathcal{O}$AT WAFFLES

60 g/2 oz old-fashioned rolled oats (see Note)
45 g/1½ oz butter, cut into pieces
175 g/6 oz plain flour
1 tablespoon caster sugar
1½ teaspoons baking powder
½ teaspoon bicarbonate of soda
½ teaspoon salt
2 size 3 eggs
250 ml/8 fl oz buttermilk

TO SERVE
Butter
Blueberry or blackcurrant preserve

In a medium saucepan, combine oats with 300 ml/½ pint water. Bring to a simmer over medium heat and cook, stirring frequently, for 3 minutes. Remove from heat and stir butter into hot porridge until melted.

Sift flour, sugar, baking powder, bicarbonate of soda and salt into a mixing bowl. In another bowl, combine eggs and buttermilk and beat lightly. Stir porridge into egg-milk mixture. Add porridge mixture to dry ingredients and stir just until well blended; do not overbeat.

Preheat waffle iron until hot. Cook waffles according to waffle iron manufacturer's directions, using about 175 ml/6 fl oz batter for each 20 cm/8 inch waffle.

Serve hot with butter and blueberry or blackcurrant preserve.

— MAKES FOUR 20 CM/8 INCH WAFFLES —

Note: Quick-cooking (but not instant) porridge oats may be used, but reduce the water to 250 ml/8 fl oz and decrease cooking time to 30 seconds before adding butter.

If buttermilk is unavailable, 175 ml/6 fl oz plain yogurt mixed with 4 tablespoons milk may be used instead.

FROSTY MORNING

MENU

◆

GRILLED UGLI FRUIT WITH CRANBERRY SAUCE

◆

BAKED BACON SPIRALS

◆

CORNMEAL GRIDDLE CAKES WITH MAPLE BUTTER

◆

MULLED APPLE SAUCE

OPPOSITE: MULLED APPLE SAUCE

GRILLED UGLI FRUIT WITH CRANBERRY SAUCE

Serve this exotic grape-fruit-tangerine hybrid in a salad as well. Peel the individual sections (the skin comes off easily) and arrange them with slices of ripe avocado on a colourful plate. Dress with a vinaigrette flavoured with orange juice.

USE A GOOD-QUALITY CRANBERRY SAUCE FOR THIS RECIPE. IF UGLI fruit are not available, substitute grapefruit.

2   ripe ugli fruit, halved and seeded
4   tablespoons cranberry sauce

Preheat grill.

Loosen ugli fruit halves with a small knife. Place on baking sheet, cut side up, and grill about 10 cm/4 inches from heat source for 3 minutes.

Remove from grill and spread each ugli fruit half with 1 tablespoon cranberry sauce. Return fruit to grill and grill for 3 minutes more, or until the cranberry sauce is hot and bubbly, being careful not to let them burn. Serve warm.

— 4 SERVINGS —

Tiny uncultivated cranberries, grown principally in Sweden, are known as lingonberries. Their natural flavour has a character often lacking in cultivated berries, and, as they hold their shape during cooking, sauces made with them have a good, firm texture.

English Country
CRANBERRY
SAUCE
Our traditional sauce
is cooked in open
copper kettles
using only small wild,
Swedish Cranberries
and sugar.

Made in England

net wt 325 g 11.5 OZ

$\mathscr{B}$AKED BACON SPIRALS

8   thick rashers lean back bacon
8   wooden cocktail sticks

Preheat oven to 200° C/400° F/Gas 6.

Roll each bacon rasher into a spiral and secure with a cocktail stick. Arrange spirals on a wire rack over a roasting pan. Place in the centre of hot oven and bake for 15 to 18 minutes, or until bacon is crisp and golden brown. Place bacon on kitchen paper to drain briefly and remove cocktails sticks.

Serve immediately.

— 4 SERVINGS —

CORNMEAL GRIDDLE CAKES WITH MAPLE BUTTER

LIGHT, MOIST AND SLIGHTLY CRUNCHY GRIDDLE CAKES BALANCE THE sweetness of the maple butter. Even better, they are easy to make, especially if the dry ingredients for the griddle cakes are sifted into the mixing bowl the night before and the butter for the maple butter is left out to soften overnight.

MAPLE BUTTER		
150 ml/¼ pint maple syrup		
125 g/4 oz butter, softened		

GRIDDLE CAKES		
85	g/scant 3 oz cornmeal	
45	g/1½ oz plain flour	
2	teaspoons baking powder	
½	teaspoon salt	
1½	tablespoons caster sugar	
1	size 3 egg	
300 ml/½ pint milk		
45	g/1½ oz butter, melted	

In a small saucepan, simmer the maple syrup over medium heat for 7 to 10 minutes, until reduced to 125 ml/4 fl oz. Remove from the heat and let cool to lukewarm. Add softened butter and stir until the mixture is creamy and well blended. Set aside at room temperature.

In a mixing bowl, combine cornmeal, flour, baking powder, salt and sugar. In another bowl, beat egg lightly, then beat in the milk. Make a well in the centre of dry ingredients and slowly stir in milk-egg mixture. Add melted butter and stir until just smooth.

Preheat a greased griddle until a few drops of cold water bounce when splashed on it. Ladle about 3 tablespoons of batter on to the griddle for each cake, leaving about 7.5 cm/3 inches between each to allow for spreading. Cook until bubbles appear on the surfaces, and undersides are golden brown, 2 to 3 minutes. Turn with a fish slice and cook until the undersides are lightly browned. Remove griddle cakes from the griddle and keep them warm while you repeat the process with remaining batter.

Serve griddle cakes hot, accompanied by maple butter.

— 4 SERVINGS (ABOUT 12 GRIDDLE CAKES) —

Mulled Apple Sauce

THE CONCENTRATED SPICED APPLE JUICE GIVES THIS apple sauce a wonderful rich fruitiness. It can be made up to three days ahead and then refrigerated until needed.

1	stick cinnamon, broken in half
3	whole cloves
3	whole allspice berries
1	2.5 cm/1 inch strip orange zest
500	ml/16 fl oz apple juice
6	to 8 tart apples (about 1.5 kg/3 lb), peeled, cored and coarsely diced
	Pinch salt
60	g/2 oz light brown sugar
60	to 100 g/2 to 3½ oz caster sugar
15	g/½ oz butter, softened

Place cinnamon, cloves, allspice and orange zest in a spice bag or in a square of muslin tied securely with string.

In a heavy saucepan, bring apple juice to the boil over high heat. Add spice bag, reduce heat to medium and simmer until juice is reduced to 150 ml/¼ pint, about 30 minutes. Remove and discard spice bag.

Add apples, salt and brown sugar to the reduced juice. Cover and simmer over medium-low heat, stirring frequently, until apples become mushy, about 20 minutes.

Taste and add enough caster sugar to bring mixture to desired sweetness. (The amount of sugar will vary with the sweetness of the apples used.) Add butter and stir until well blended.

Serve warm or lightly chilled.

— MAKES 1 LITRE/1¾ PINTS —

This maple cream sauce, a delicious alternative for the cornmeal griddle cakes, is rich and smooth and pours like cream. In a small saucepan, heat 150 ml/¼ pint maple syrup, 125 ml/4 fl oz double cream, and 90 g/ 3 oz butter, stirring, until the butter is melted, then simmer the mixture over low heat for 10 minutes, or until it is slightly thickened. Let the sauce stand until just warm and stir it well before serving. Makes about 250 ml/8 fl oz.

COUNTRY WEEKEND BREAKFAST

MENU

◆

*T*INY FRUITS WITH MINT AND CRÈME FRAÎCHE SAUCE

◆

*A*MERICAN-STYLE MARMALADE MUFFINS

◆

*E*GGS BAKED IN DILL CRÊPE NESTS

◆

*F*RIZZLED HAM STRIPS ON WATERCRESS

OPPOSITE: AMERICAN-STYLE MARMALADE MUFFINS, TINY FRUITS WITH MINT AND CRÈME FRAÎCHE SAUCE, EGGS BAKED IN DILL CRÊPE NESTS, AND FRIZZLED HAM STRIPS ON WATERCRESS

To make crème fraîche, *mix 250 ml/8 fl oz soured cream with 250 to 500 ml /8 to 16 fl oz fresh double cream (do not use UHT cream).*

Let the mixture stand, unrefrigerated, for several hours, or until it is thickened. Cover and refrigerate.

Crème fraîche *will keep for several days and can be used in place of soured cream or whenever a slightly tart flavour is desired.*

$\mathcal{T}$INY FRUITS WITH MINT AND CRÈME FRAÎCHE SAUCE

250 ml/8 fl oz *crème fraîche* (see Note)
2 tablespoons double cream
2 tablespoons chopped fresh mint leaves, or
 1 teaspoon dried mint
3 to 4 tablespoons icing sugar
250 g/8 oz berries or grapes, preferably a mixture of
 raspberries, strawberries, blueberries, and red and
 green grapes

TO SERVE
Fresh mint sprigs

In a small mixing bowl, combine *crème fraîche*, double cream, chopped mint and icing sugar. If mixture is too thick, add more double cream. If it's not sweet enough, add more icing sugar. Spoon into a decorative serving dish and set aside.

Combine fruit in a large bowl and mix. Divide between 4 individual serving plates or shallow dishes. Garnish with mint sprigs.

Spoon a mound of the *crème fraîche* sauce on to each serving plate next to the fruit and serve remaining sauce separately.

— 4 SERVINGS —

Note: If *crème fraîche* is unavailable, soured cream can be substituted, and the double cream, which is added to thin the *crème fraîche* slightly, can be omitted.

AMERICAN-STYLE MARMALADE MUFFINS

ANY THICK JAM OR PRESERVE CAN BE USED IN PLACE OF THE MAR-malade, but these are especially pretty when a variety of colourful marmalades and preserves fills the muffins.

250 g/8 oz plain flour
1   tablespoon baking powder
½   teaspoon bicarbonate of soda
2   tablespoons caster sugar
2   tablespoons light brown sugar
½   teaspoon salt
1   size 3 egg
250 ml/8 fl oz milk
60 g/2 oz butter, melted and cooled
1   tablespoon grated orange zest
6   tablespoons orange or lemon marmalade or other fruit preserve

Preheat oven to 200° C/400° F/Gas 6.

In a large mixing bowl, sift flour, baking powder, bicarbonate of soda, caster sugar, brown sugar and salt together. In a separate bowl, beat egg lightly, then beat in the milk. Mix butter and orange zest into egg-milk mixture. Make a well in the centre of dry ingredients and add liquid mixture all at once. Using a large wooden spoon, stir batter with 10 to 15 swift strokes, or until ingredients are just combined. Do not overmix; batter should remain slightly lumpy.

Spoon about 2 tablespoons of batter into the bottom of each of 12 generously greased deep bun tins. Add 1½ teaspoons marmalade to each tin. Then add enough additional batter to fill each three-quarters full.

Bake in the centre of oven for 18 to 20 minutes, or until muffins are golden brown and a skewer inserted into centres comes out free of batter. Turn out of tins on to a wire rack to cool slightly. Serve warm.

— MAKES 12 MUFFINS —

Marmalade, as much a part of the British breakfast ritual as a cup of tea, takes its name from marmelo, Portuguese for 'quince' (because marmalades before the eighteenth century were usually sweet quince pastes). Today, they are almost always made from citrus fruits in a wide variety of combinations: even the simplest British orange marmalades range from lightly flavoured ones made with sweet oranges and finely sliced rinds to dark, sharper-tasting varieties made with bitter, or Seville, oranges and thick chunky pieces of rind.

Simple crêpes–the makings of Pancake Day, or Shrove Tuesday–were once the final extravagance before Lent. Sprinkle sugar and enough fresh lemon juice on each crêpe to sharpen the taste and roll the crêpe up. Arrange on a warm serving plate with lemon wedges and the leaves and lemon-coloured blossoms of primroses, if available.

$\mathscr{E}$GGS BAKED IN DILL CRÊPE NESTS

CRÊPES MAY BE MADE IN ADVANCE AND KEPT IN THE REFRIGERATOR overnight or frozen. To store, stack them between pieces of greaseproof paper and place in a polythene bag. Serve any unused crêpes at another meal, filled with vegetables, meat or fish in a sauce.

CRÊPES	
75	g/2½ oz plain flour
⅛	teaspoon salt
⅛	teaspoon white pepper
125 ml/4 fl oz milk	
1	whole size 3 egg
1	size 3 egg yolk
1	tablespoon chopped fresh dill, or 1 teaspoon dried dill
25	g/¾ oz butter, melted

BAKED EGGS	
8	size 3 eggs
	Salt
	Freshly ground black pepper
45	g/1½ oz butter, melted
8	sprigs fresh dill

In a large mixing bowl, combine flour, salt and white pepper. Make a well in the centre of dry ingredients. Combine milk with 3 tablespoons water and stir gradually into dry ingredients. In a small bowl, beat whole egg and yolk together lightly. Add eggs to batter, along with the dill and butter. Stir just until blended. Let rest for 1 to 2 hours.

To prepare crêpes, heat a lightly greased 12.5 to 13 cm/5 to 5½ inch crêpe pan over medium-high heat until beads of water sizzle when dropped on the surface. Stir crêpe batter, then ladle 1½ to 2 tablespoons batter into the pan and swirl to coat surface completely. Cook until bottom of crêpe is lightly browned, 30 to 45 seconds. Turn with a fish slice and brown the other side for 15 to 20 seconds. Turn on to a wire rack to cool, then stack on a plate between layers of greaseproof paper. Continue in this manner until all crêpe batter is used, adding more butter to the pan as needed.

Preheat oven to 180°C/350° F/Gas 4.

Ease 1 crêpe into each of 8 generously buttered deep bun tins, gently ruffling edges. Bake in the centre of the oven 8 minutes. Break an egg into each crêpe cup and season each with salt and black pepper. Bake for 7 to 9 minutes, or until whites of eggs are set but yolks are still runny. Remove from the oven and, using both hands, carefully lift crêpe cups from tins on to serving plates. Drizzle about 1 teaspoon butter over each egg and garnish with dill. Serve immediately.

— 4 TO 8 SERVINGS (8 CRÊPES) —

ℱRIZZLED HAM STRIPS ON WATERCRESS

175 g/6 oz lightly smoked ham, cut into 3 mm/⅛ inch
    thick slices
30 g/1 oz unsalted butter
2 teaspoons blackcurrant or raspberry vinegar
1 large bunch watercress, stalks removed
    Salt
    Freshly ground pepper

Cut ham slices into 4 cm × 5 mm/1½ × ¼ inch strips. In a medium frying pan, melt half of the butter. Add ham strips and sauté over medium-high heat, tossing gently, for 3 to 4 minutes, or until golden brown, slightly curled and crispy. Remove ham strips and keep them warm.

Add vinegar to the pan and swirl to deglaze. Add remaining butter and melt. Add watercress and sauté over medium-high heat, tossing gently, for 30 to 45 seconds, or until it begins to wilt. Remove from heat, season with salt and pepper and toss.

Arrange watercress on a warmed serving platter. Top with ham strips and serve immediately.

— 4 SERVINGS —

In summer, substitute sorrel for watercress. Tear tender sorrel leaves into roughly 2.5 cm/ 1 inch square pieces before adding them to the juices in the pan, preferably a non-reactive pan to prevent the leaves from darkening.

FOR THE EARLY-RISING FISHERMAN

MENU

◆

*S*TRAWBERRIES
WITH STRAWBERRY
VINEGAR

◆

*H*OME-SMOKED TROUT
WITH ROSEMARY

◆

*P*OTATO PANCAKES
WITH CHILLI RELISH

OPPOSITE: HOME-SMOKED TROUT WITH
ROSEMARY

Salmo gairdneri irideus — male in the spawning season

The Rainbow Trout

Salmo gairdneri irideus Gibbons 1855

STRAWBERRIES WITH STRAWBERRY VINEGAR

THE BERRIES MUST BE UTTERLY RIPE AND VERY SWEET; THEIR FLAVOUR and aroma are then heightened by the vinegar. They are also best served at room temperature, so that their fragrance is released.

600 g/1¼ lb ripe strawberries with stalks
2   to 3 tablespoons strawberry vinegar

Shortly before serving, rinse berries briefly in cold water, drain and pat dry with kitchen paper.

Arrange berries in a shallow serving bowl. Sprinkle with the vinegar and serve. No utensils are needed; pick up berries by the stalks to eat.

— 4 SERVINGS —

Line the serving bowl with strawberry leaves, if available, to make a fresh background for the berries. Then sprinkle a few drops of rosewater over the berries just before serving. Strawberries and roses belong to the same botanical family, and their aromas complement each other wonderfully.

Strawberry
RED WINE
VINEGAR

Crabtree & Evelyn
LONDON

For Salad Dressings

6° ACETIC ACID

MADE IN FRANCE
370 ml 13 oz fl

*H*OME-SMOKED TROUT
WITH ROSEMARY

THE TROUT IS SOAKED IN BRINE FOR A DAY BEFORE IT IS COOKED AND should be smoked in a covered barbecue. Serve the trout warm, soon after smoking.

2   whole 250 to 300 g/8 to 10 oz fresh trout, cleaned
4   tablespoons sea salt
     Hickory chips or other wood chips for barbecuing
2   sprigs fresh rosemary

ROSEMARY BUTTER
45   g/1½ oz unsalted butter, softened
1   teaspoon finely chopped fresh rosemary, or ½ teaspoon dried

To soak, rinse trout thoroughly in water, place in a 3 litre/5 pint enamel or other non-reactive pan and add salt and 2 litres/3½ pints water. The fish should be completely covered with brine. Cover and refrigerate for 24 hours.

Place 2 to 3 handfuls of hickory chips in a basin of cold water and soak for 30 minutes. About an hour before serving the fish, build an indirect barbecue fire by placing the charcoal to one side of the fire basket of the barbecue. When the charcoal becomes grey-white, drain the hickory chips and toss them on to the coals. Oil the grid, cover the barbecue, and leave the fire for 5 to 10 minutes.

Remove trout from brine, drain and rinse under cold water. Using a sharp knife, remove heads and slit down the centre along back bone on inside to butterfly each trout.

Place trout, skin side down, on the grid away from the hot coals so that they cook over indirect heat. Lay fresh rosemary sprigs on the fish. Cover barbecue and let trout smoke for about 40 minutes, or until the flesh is cooked through.

In a small bowl, combine butter and chopped rosemary and beat until blended.

Remove trout from the barbecue. Cut each in half lengthways and serve topped with knobs of the rosemary butter.

— 4 BREAKFAST SERVINGS —

As a lunch or dinner dish, this trout is excellent served with a piquant horseradish sauce made by stirring 2 to 4 tablespoons Crabtree & Evelyn Horseradish Sauce into 125 ml/4 fl oz soured cream or crème fraîche.

POTATO PANCAKES WITH CHILLI RELISH

Potato pancakes are delicious served with poached eggs. Drain the eggs very well, place one on each pancake, and spoon the relish on top. The relish is also a fine accompaniment to scrambled or fried eggs and a colourful filling for an omelet.

IF ANY OF THE CHILLIES ARE UNAVAILABLE, SUBSTITUTE HALF A SMALL green, yellow or red pepper for the chilli of the same colour in the recipe. The relish should be brightly coloured and also have some bite, so use the Tabasco sauce to strike the right balance of hotness, depending on the heat of the chillies. Also, the relish can be made the night before and reheated at the last minute.

CHILLI RELISH
1	tablespoon vegetable oil
1	fresh green chilli, cored, seeded and finely chopped
1	small yellow chilli, cored, seeded and finely chopped
1	small mild red chilli, cored, seeded and finely chopped
2	tablespoons thinly sliced spring onion
2	tablespoons white wine vinegar
	Several drops Tabasco or other hot pepper sauce (optional)
	Salt
	Freshly ground black pepper

POTATO PANCAKES
1	size 3 egg
1	tablespoon plain flour
¼	teaspoon salt
	Pinch freshly ground black pepper
2	large all-purpose potatoes (about 500 g/1 lb), peeled, coarsely grated and set aside in a bowl of cold water
15	to 30 g/½ to 1 oz butter
1	tablespoon vegetable oil

To prepare the relish, heat oil in a medium frying pan. Add green, yellow and red chillies and spring onion and sauté over medium heat for about 3 minutes. Turn mixture into a small bowl. Return pan to the heat, add vinegar and swirl for 30 seconds over medium heat to deglaze. Pour vinegar into chilli-onion mixture. Let cool slightly and taste. Season with Tabasco, if desired, salt and pepper. Set aside.

In a mixing bowl, combine egg, flour, salt and black pepper and beat together lightly. Drain potatoes in a colander and pat dry with kitchen paper. Add potatoes to egg batter and toss until well coated.

Preheat oven to 95° C/200° F/Gas ¼.

In a large frying pan, heat half the butter and oil over medium-high heat until hot. Spoon about one quarter of potato mixture into the pan and flatten into a 12.5 cm/5 inch pancake. Spoon another quarter of the mixture into the pan, allowing a few inches between the 2 pancakes, and flatten. Cook over medium heat for 5 minutes, or until the bottoms are lightly browned. Carefully turn the pancakes with a fish slice and cook until the other sides are lightly browned and pancakes are cooked through. Transfer pancakes to a baking sheet and place in the oven to keep warm. Use remaining batter and remaining butter and oil to make two more 12.5 cm/5 inch potato pancakes in the same manner.

Spoon a little relish on each pancake and serve.

— 4 SERVINGS —

For a fine accompaniment to roasted meats and fish dishes, vary this potato pancakes recipe by using only 1 large potato and substituting an equal quantity of raw turnip for the second potato. Treat both vegetables in the same way as the potatoes in the recipe, but make the mixture into 8 smaller pancakes instead of the 4 suggested.

BRUNCH

INTERMEZZO

MENU

◆

CRANBERRY-ORANGE JUICE

◆

SCRAMBLED EGGS WITH CHEDDAR AND CHIVES

◆

PEPPERY CORNMEAL BUNS

◆

SIMPLE SAUSAGE PATTIES

◆

AROMATIC PEARS

OPPOSITE: AROMATIC PEAR AND
CRANBERRY-ORANGE JUICE

CRANBERRY-ORANGE JUICE

USE THE SWEETEST, RIPEST ORANGES AVAILABLE.

1.5 litres/2½ pints cranberry juice	TO SERVE
1.75ml/6 fl oz freshly squeezed orange juice	6 orange slices

Combine cranberry and orange juices in a jug and stir to blend well. Chill until serving time.

Pour into 6 tall glasses filled with ice cubes. Garnish the rim of each glass with an orange slice.

— 6 SERVINGS —

SCRAMBLED EGGS
WITH CHEDDAR AND CHIVES

THE CHEESE THAT FALLS ON THE SCRAMBLED EGGS MELTS ON THE WAY to the table; the rest stays whole, in feathery strands over the top. Serve the eggs in a warm serving dish or from the pan in which they have cooked and pass the salt separately, as the Cheddar may well have added enough saltiness to the dish.

It is worth seeking out mature farmhouse Cheddar, as its deep nutty flavour will season more assertively than the milder, young Cheddars that are more generally available.

12	size 3 eggs	2	to 3 tablespoons snipped
5½	tablespoons milk		chives or finely sliced spring
2	teaspoons whole-grain mustard		onion tops
45	g/1½ oz unsalted butter		Freshly ground pepper
175	g/6 oz mature Cheddar cheese, grated		Salt (optional)

In a large mixing bowl, combine eggs, milk and mustard and beat together lightly.

In a large frying pan, melt butter. Add eggs and cook over low heat, stirring almost constantly, until they have formed into a creamy mass but are not yet completely set; eggs should not be dry.

Carefully slide the eggs on to a warm serving platter, or finish preparing and serve from the pan. Sprinkle eggs with grated cheese. Scatter chives over cheese and top with a generous grind of pepper and salt, if desired. Serve immediately.

— 6 SERVINGS —

PEPPERY CORNMEAL BUNS

IN THE UNITED STATES, THESE BUNS ARE MADE IN THE SHAPE OF CORN-on-the-cob, using special heavy cast-iron cornstick moulds. If you have one of these moulds, by all means use it. Increase the oven temperature to 220° C/425° F/Gas 7 and bake for 9 to 11 minutes.

	Bacon fat or margarine, melted
125	g/4 oz cornmeal
140	g/5 oz plain flour
2	tablespoons caster sugar
4	teaspoons baking powder
½	teaspoon salt
½	teaspoon freshly ground white pepper
1	size 3 egg
250	ml/8 fl oz milk
60	g/2 oz unsalted butter, melted

Preheat oven to 200° C/400° F/Gas 6.

Brush 12 deep bun tins lightly with bacon fat and heat in the oven while making batter.

Sift cornmeal, flour, sugar, baking powder, salt and pepper into a large mixing bowl. In a small bowl, beat the egg lightly, then beat in the milk and butter. Make a well in the centre of dry ingredients, add egg-milk mixture and stir just to combine.

Remove hot bun tins from oven and fill each with about 2½ table-spoons batter.

Return tins to hot oven and bake for about 20 minutes, or until buns are cooked through and lightly browned on top. Lift buns out of tins with a small knife, place in a napkin-lined basket and serve warm.

— MAKES 12 BUNS —

Crumbled cornmeal buns or corn bread can be used in place of any other bread (usually white) to make an excellent stuffing for chicken or turkey.

$\mathcal{S}$IMPLE SAUSAGE PATTIES

SAGE AND PEPPER ARE TRADITIONAL FLAVOURINGS IN FARMHOUSE sausage meat. If this is prepared a day ahead, the flavours mingle beautifully.

The pork should have about a 30 per cent fat content and can be minced in b tches in a mincer (use the plate with 9 mm/⅜ inch holes) or a food processor.

1	kg/2 lb boneless lean pork, cut into 4 cm/1½ inch cubes
1	small clove garlic
1¼	teaspoons sea salt
2	teaspoons finely chopped fresh sage leaves, or ¾ teaspoon dried
2	teaspoons coarsely ground black pepper
¼	teaspoon cayenne pepper
	Pinch grated nutmeg
15	to 30 g/½ to 1 oz butter

For variety, substitute ¾ teaspoon dried oregano or 1 teaspoon fennel seeds for the sage.

Freeze pork in a single layer on a baking sheet for about 45 minutes, or until meat is partially frozen. Working with a quarter of the pork at a time, pulse the meat in a food processor until coarsely minced and crumbly.

Finely chop and mash garlic and salt together on a cutting board to form a paste. In a large mixing bowl, combine garlic-salt paste, sage, black pepper, cayenne and nutmeg. Add minced meat to the spice mixture and, using fingertips or a wooden spoon, combine the pork thoroughly with seasonings. Chill in the refrigerator for at least 1 hour to allow flavours to blend and intensify.

To check seasoning, fry a small piece of the sausage mixture well before serving time and taste. Correct seasoning if necessary.

Shortly before serving, shape meat into 6 cm/2½ inch patties. Melt butter in a large frying pan over medium-low heat. Add several patties and cook for 4 to 6 minutes on each side, or until patties are crisp and browned on the outside and no longer pink inside. Place patties on a warm serving platter and keep them warm while you prepare remaining patties. Serve hot.

— 6 SERVINGS (ABOUT 12 PATTIES) —

Aromatic Pears

THE FRAGRANCE OF THIS DISH SHARPENS THE APPETITE FOR THE warmer flavours of autumn and winter cooking. The pears are most elegantly served at room temperature or chilled but are also excellent eaten warm for supper on a cold night.

Small pears were used to make this recipe, but six standard-size pears may be used instead. Larger pears may need 10 to 15 minutes more cooking, unless they are very ripe.

1	lemon	TO SERVE
250	ml/8 fl oz dry white wine	250 ml/8 fl oz double cream,
60	g/2 oz caster sugar	whipped to soft peaks
½	vanilla pod	and chilled
1	stick cinnamon	
2	whole cloves	
⅛	teaspoon ground ginger	
12	firm-fleshed dessert pears (1 to 1.25 kg/2 to 2½ lb)	

Grate zest from the lemon with a sharp hand grater and set aside. Halve lemon, extract 1 tablespoon juice and set lemon halves and juice aside.

In a large, heavy saucepan, combine lemon zest, wine, sugar, vanilla pod, cinnamon stick, cloves, ginger and 500 ml/16 fl oz water. Bring mixture to the boil over medium-high heat. Lower heat to medium-low and simmer syrup for about 5 minutes.

Meanwhile peel pears with a vegetable peeler, leaving stalks on. Rub the surfaces of the pears with the cut side of a lemon half to prevent them from darkening. Poach pears in the syrup until tender, 10 to 20 minutes, stirring and turning pears 2 or 3 times so that they cook evenly. (Pears are cooked when their flesh can be pierced easily with the tip of a knife.) Remove from heat and let pears cool in syrup for about 10 minutes.

Using a slotted spoon, remove pears from syrup and arrange them, stalk ends up, in a shallow serving dish. Return syrup to the boil over high heat until reduced to 350 ml/12 fl oz. Stir in lemon juice. Remove syrup from heat and let cool to lukewarm.

Carefully strain syrup over pears. Serve pears accompanied by whipped cream in a separate bowl.

— 6 SERVINGS —

For a gingery, robust syrup for these pears, replace the sugar and ground ginger with 5 tablespoons Crabtree & Evelyn Honey & Ginger Sauce. Its warm spiciness sets off the coolness of the pears.

FOREIGN EXCHANGE

M E N U

◆

*S*AGE AND GRUYÈRE
OMELETS

◆

*S*PINACH, APPLE AND
WALNUT SALAD

◆

*B*RAISED SAUERKRAUT
AND BRATWURST

◆

*S*YLLABUB

◆

*M*OLASSES BISCUITS

OPPOSITE: SPINACH, APPLE AND
WALNUT SALAD

ＳAGE AND GRUYÈRE OMELETS

EACH OMELET TAKES LESS THAN A MINUTE TO MAKE. THE QUANTITIES can be adjusted to increase or decrease the number of servings, but, as omelets should be eaten immediately, it is usually impractical to cook them for more than four people at a time.

8	size 3 eggs	30	g/1 oz unsalted butter
2	teaspoons chopped fresh sage leaves, or ¾ teaspoon dried sage	60	g/2 oz Gruyère cheese, grated
	Salt		TO SERVE
	Freshly ground pepper	4	sprigs fresh sage (optional)

Crack eggs into a large mixing bowl. Add sage, salt and pepper and beat lightly with a fork.

In a 17.5 or 20 cm/7 or 8 inch omelet pan or heavy frying pan, melt 15 g/½ oz of the butter over medium-high heat until foamy. When foam subsides, add a quarter of the egg mixture and swirl pan to distribute evenly. As eggs begin to set, lift edge gently with a fork and tilt pan to allow uncooked eggs to run underneath. When eggs are nearly set but still very moist, after about 40 seconds, sprinkle a quarter of the grated cheese across the centre of the omelet. Gently fold omelet in half with a palette knife and slide it on to a warm serving plate.

Repeat process with remaining eggs and cheese to make three more individual omelets, adding more butter as needed. Garnish each omelet with a sprig of fresh sage, if desired, and serve immediately.

— 4 SERVINGS —

With its distinctive flavour and creamy texture when melted, Gruyère is one of the best cooking cheeses. Try it folded into scrambled eggs (topped with fried croûtons), on pasta, in cheese bread puddings, in deep-fried cheese squares and fritters, and in combination with freshly grated Parmesan in soufflés, gratin toppings and cream sauces. And, to appreciate Gruyère at its best when eaten with fruit, cut the cheese into very thin slices with a slotted cheese slicer.

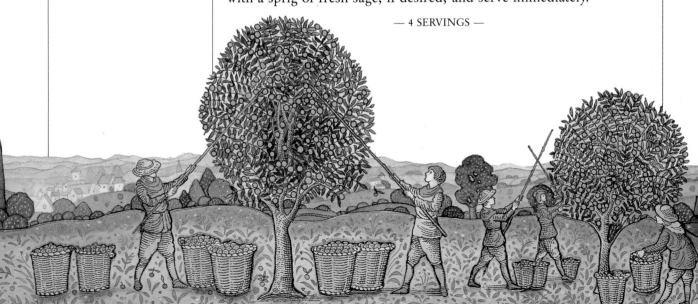

$\mathcal{S}$PINACH, APPLE AND WALNUT SALAD

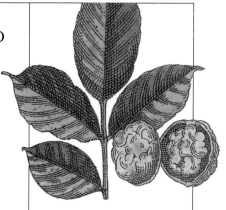

30 g/1 oz shelled walnuts, broken or coarsely chopped

DRESSING
4 tablespoons walnut oil
4 tablespoons vegetable oil
2 tablespoons blackcurrant wine vinegar or other fruit-flavoured wine vinegar
   Salt
   Freshly ground pepper

TO SERVE
300 g/10 oz fresh spinach leaves, washed, dried and stalks removed
1 Red Delicious apple, cored but not peeled
1 teaspoon lemon juice

Preheat oven to 180° C/350° F/Gas 4.

Spread walnuts on a baking sheet and bake until lightly toasted and fragrant, 5 to 8 minutes, watching carefully to prevent burning. Turn the oven off but keep walnuts warm in the oven until needed.

In a small bowl, whisk together walnut oil, vegetable oil and vinegar. Season with salt and pepper and whisk until blended.

Tear spinach leaves into bite-size pieces and place in a large salad bowl. Slice apple as thinly as possible, sprinkle with lemon juice and add to salad bowl. Add vinaigrette and toss to coat spinach and apples well. Divide salad among 4 salad plates and sprinkle each portion with toasted nuts.

— 4 SERVINGS —

When spinach leaves are tender and small, make the salad into a centre-piece for your table. Snip away the stalks and arrange the leaves, stalk ends down, in a shallow salad bowl in concentric circles so that the salad has the look of a huge flower. Mix the apple slices with the dressing and spoon the mixture into the centre of the leaves. Sprinkle the rest of the dressing over the spinach leaves, and the nuts on top of the apples.

BRAISED SAUERKRAUT AND BRATWURST

THIS DISH CAN BE PREPARED AHEAD TO THE POINT WHERE THE SAUsages are added to the sauerkraut. Other mild sausages may be used instead of bratwurst, in which case omit the bacon fat for sautéeing.

The braised sauerkraut, without sausage added, makes a fine accompaniment for roast duck or pheasant.

4	bratwurst sausages (about 350 g/12 oz)
2	tablespoons melted bacon fat
1	small onion, chopped
500 g/1 lb	sauerkraut, rinsed and drained well
4	tablespoons apple juice
4	tablespoons dry white wine
1	bay leaf
4	whole juniper berries
¼	teaspoon dried thyme
	Freshly ground pepper
	Salt (optional)

In a large, heavy frying pan, sauté sausages in bacon fat until golden brown and just heated through, about 10 minutes. Remove from pan and set aside. Pour off all but 1 tablespoon pan drippings.

Add onion to pan and sauté over medium heat until softened and translucent, about 4 minutes. Stir in sauerkraut, apple juice and wine. Break bay leaf in half and add to pan. Crush juniper berries slightly and add, along with thyme. Season generously with pepper and stir until well mixed. Cover pan and simmer over medium-low heat for about 15 minutes. Taste sauerkraut for seasoning and add salt, if desired. Arrange sausages on top of sauerkraut. Partially cover pan and simmer over medium-low heat for 5 to 10 minutes longer, or until sausages are heated through. Discard bay leaf halves.

Transfer to a platter or divide among individual plates and serve immediately.

— 4 SERVINGS —

Syllabub

THIS IRRESISTIBLE DESSERT SHOULD BE MADE THE DAY IT IS TO BE eaten. Sherry is often used in place of the white wine, and either version makes a superb filling for the Molasses-Rum Lace Wafers on page 227.

2	lemons
5½	tablespoons white wine
1	to 2 tablespoons brandy
5½	tablespoons caster sugar
250	ml/8 fl oz double cream

FOR DECORATION
4   sprigs fresh mint or 4 strips of lemon zest (optional)

Carefully remove the zest from the lemons, avoiding the pith as much as possible. In a bowl, combine 4 tablespoons juice from the lemons with the zest, reserving 4 strips for decoration if desired, the wine, brandy and sugar and set aside for at least 3 hours.

Strain the mixture through a sieve into a larger bowl and discard the zest. With a wire whisk or electric hand mixer set at low, beat the lemon mixture while slowly pouring in the cream and continue beating for 2 to 3 minutes, or until the syllabub is just thick enough to hold the marks of the whisk. Divide the syllabub among 4 bowls or glasses, cover with cling film and refrigerate.

Before serving, decorate with the mint or the lemon zest.

— 4 SERVINGS —

This perennial English favourite combines the creamiest of textures with a sharp, refreshing taste. Syllabub has been known for centuries and in its simplest form was made by directing milk straight from the cow's udder into a bowl of cider or wine.

*M*OLASSES BISCUITS

When measuring molasses, lightly butter or oil the measuring jug; the molasses then slides from the jug without sticking to the sides. This also increases the accuracy of the measuring. Alternatively, you can weigh the quantity of molasses required if your scales can accommodate the mixing bowl. Weigh out 165 g/5½ oz molasses.

THESE SPICY, SLIGHTLY SOFT BISCUITS ARE DELICIOUS WITH A LIGHT mousse, ice cream or fresh fruit.

280 g/10 oz plain flour
½ teaspoon bicarbonate of soda
½ teaspoon salt
1 teaspoon ground cinnamon
½ teaspoon ground ginger
150 g/5 oz caster sugar
125 g/4 oz unsalted butter, softened
125 ml/4 fl oz molasses
1 size 3 egg, lightly beaten
1 tablespoon grated fresh root ginger

Sift flour, bicarbonate of soda, salt, cinnamon and ground ginger together on a sheet of greaseproof paper and set aside.

In a large mixing bowl, cream together 100 g/3½ oz of the sugar and the butter until light and fluffy. Add molasses, egg and root ginger and beat until light. Gradually add the flour, stirring until well blended. Cover dough and chill for at least 1 hour or overnight.

Preheat oven to 180° C/350° F/Gas 4.

Form dough into 2.5 cm/1 inch balls, rolling them between the palms until smooth and round. Spread remaining sugar on greaseproof paper and roll each ball of dough in sugar. Place dough balls 5 cm/2 inches apart on greased baking sheets. Bake in the centre of hot oven until tops are rounded and crinkled and cookies are just beginning to colour, about 12 to 14 minutes. Remove from the oven and transfer to wire racks to cool. Store in a tightly covered container.

— MAKES ABOUT 32 BISCUITS —

COUNTRY PURSUITS

M E N U

◆

ARTICHOKES WITH
LEMON-HERB SAUCE

◆

COUNTRY HAM AND
POTATO FRITTATA

◆

OAT BUTTERMILK
QUICK BREAD

◆

PLUM PRESERVE
BUTTER

◆

TROPICAL FRUIT
COMPOTE

OPPOSITE: COUNTRY HAM AND POTATO
FRITTATA AND ARTICHOKES WITH
LEMON-HERB SAUCE

Artichokes with Lemon-Herb Sauce

THE ARTICHOKES MAY BE SERVED WARM, OR THEY MAY BE CHILLED IN the refrigerator for up to 8 hours and eaten cold. The sauce can be made up to 2 days ahead and chilled. Either way, fill the artichokes just before serving.

This light sauce is also excellent poured over tiny boiled new potatoes, green beans or broccoli.

6 medium globe artichokes
½ lemon
½ teaspoon salt

LEMON-HERB SAUCE
1 size 3 egg
2 teaspoons whole-grain mustard
1 to 1½ tablespoons fresh lemon juice
175 ml/6 fl oz vegetable oil
1 teaspoon grated lemon zest
2 tablespoons finely chopped fresh chives

1 tablespoon finely chopped fresh parsley
Salt
Freshly ground pepper

TO SERVE
Lemon wedges

Trim artichokes, cutting off stalks at base, removing tough outer leaves, and using kitchen scissors to cut off spiky points of remaining leaves. Rinse under cold water. Rub cut side of lemon over cut edges of artichokes to prevent darkening.

Set artichokes, stalk ends down, in a saucepan large enough to hold all 6 artichokes without crowding. Slowly add 5 cm/2 inches water. Add salt and squeeze remaining juice from lemon half into pan. Cover and bring liquid to the boil. Lower heat to medium-low and steam artichokes, covered, for 25 to 30 minutes, or until bottoms are tender enough to be pierced easily with a knife. Remove artichokes from the pan with tongs and invert on a flat surface to drain. Let drain until cool enough to handle.

Meanwhile prepare sauce. Break egg into food processor or large mixing bowl. Add mustard and lemon juice and process or beat until blended. With processor motor running, dribble in oil through feed tube in a slow steady stream. If preparing by hand, add a few drops of oil at a time, whisking vigorously between each addition, until mixture begins to thicken. Add remaining oil in a slow steady stream, whisking constantly until all oil is incorporated. Scrape down sides of processor or bowl with a spatula, add lemon zest, chives and parsley. Season to taste with salt and pepper and blend well.

Gently pull apart inner leaves of each artichoke until you see the tender, pale green, cone-shaped leaves at centre. Remove and discard these inner leaves. Using a small spoon, carefully scrape out and discard the fuzzy choke at the centre of each artichoke. Arrange artichokes on a large serving platter. Spoon 2 to 3 tablespoons of sauce into the centre cavity of each artichoke. Arrange lemon wedges around artichokes. Place any remaining sauce in a sauceboat and serve separately.

— 6 SERVINGS —

$\mathcal{O}$AT BUTTERMILK QUICK BREAD

THIS BREAD CAN BE FROZEN OR MADE UP TO THREE DAYS BEFORE IT IS needed and stored in the refrigerator; it is more easily cut when cold. To serve, slice it into 1 cm/½ inch thick slices and arrange in a basket. Cover well and let the bread come to room temperature. Eat it with Plum Preserve Butter (page 57) or plain butter and a selection of preserves.

140 g/5 oz plain flour	90 g/3 oz honey
90 g/3 oz wholemeal flour	350 ml/12 fl oz buttermilk
1 teaspoon baking powder	60 g/2 oz butter, melted and cooled
½ teaspoon bicarbonate of soda	60 g/2 oz rolled oats (not instant)
½ teaspoon salt	90 g/3 oz currants
1 size 3 egg	

Preheat oven to 180° C/350° F/Gas 4.

Sift plain flour, wholemeal flour, baking powder, bicarbonate of soda and salt together on to a sheet of greaseproof paper. In a large mixing bowl, combine egg, honey, buttermilk and butter and beat together lightly. Stir in oats and currants. Add flour mixture all at once and stir until just blended; do not overmix. (Batter will be quite stiff.)

Line the bottom of a greased medium loaf tin with parchment or greaseproof paper. Pour batter into the pan and smooth top with a spatula. Bake in the centre of hot oven for 60 to 65 minutes, or until top of bread is deep golden brown and a skewer inserted into the centre comes out clean. Let cool in the tin for 10 minutes, then turn out on to a wire rack, removing paper lining from bread, and let cool completely. Wrap in polythene or aluminium foil and refrigerate until well chilled.

— MAKES 1 LOAF (ABOUT 14 SLICES) —

If the honey has hardened in the cupboard, stand the jar, uncovered, in a saucepan of barely simmering water for 15 to 20 minutes, or until the honey softens. Or leave it in a warm place overnight.

COUNTRY HAM AND POTATO FRITTATA

THE COMBINATION OF THE HAM SQUARES AND POTATO SLICES WITH the parsley and eggs gives this dish a colourful mosaic pattern when cut. For brunch, serve it hot, spooned out of the dish; or warm, cut into squares. Cold, the frittata is excellent picnic fare.

2	medium waxy potatoes, unpeeled
10	size 3 eggs
4	tablespoons chopped fresh parsley
3	tablespoons olive oil
1	small onion, peeled and thinly sliced
250	g/8 oz cooked well-flavoured ham such as York ham, thinly sliced and cut into 2.5 cm/1 inch squares
60	g/2 oz Parmesan or Gruyère cheese, grated Freshly ground pepper, to taste

Place potatoes in a saucepan of lightly salted boiling water and boil until just tender. Drain and set aside to cool. Break eggs into a large mixing bowl and beat until well mixed but not frothy. Stir in parsley.

Preheat oven to 200° C/400° F/Gas 6.

Pour oil into a 2 litre/3½ pint square or oval baking dish and swirl to coat bottom of dish evenly. Scatter onion slices evenly over bottom of dish. Place in hot oven for 10 minutes, or until onion slices are softened and just beginning to brown. Meanwhile slice potatoes thinly.

Remove baking dish from oven and reduce temperature to 190° C/375° F/Gas 5. Arrange ham in a single layer on top of onion. Arrange potatoes in one layer over ham. Pour in the eggs and sprinkle cheese evenly over the top. Season with pepper. (The ham is usually quite salty, so the frittata should need no added salt.)

Return baking dish to oven and bake for 25 to 30 minutes, or until eggs are set and the frittata is puffed and lightly browned on top. Serve hot, warm or cold.

— 6 SERVINGS —

Plum Preserve Butter

FRUITED BUTTERS CAN BE MADE WITH ALMOST ANY WELL-flavoured preserve, using the same proportions as below. If using marmalades omit the lemon juice.

175 g/6 oz unsalted butter, softened
3   tablespoons plum preserve
1½ teaspoons lemon juice

In a food processor or small mixing bowl, combine butter, preserve and lemon juice and process or beat until well blended. Transfer to a small crock or serving dish, cover and refrigerate until well chilled.

Remove from the refrigerator about 1 hour before serving so that butter is spreadable.

— MAKES ABOUT 250 G/8 OZ —

Tropical Fruit Compote

IF THE PINEAPPLE IS VERY RIPE, THIS COMPOTE WILL NEED NO SUGAR. The cook's reward is to eat the bits of sweet mango that cling to the stone.

1   medium-sized ripe pineapple, peeled and cored
1   ripe papaya, peeled, halved and seeded
1   ripe mango, peeled and stoned
2   ripe bananas
4   tablespoons dry white wine
1   tablespoon dark rum
     Caster sugar, if desired

To check the ripeness of a pineapple, pull one of the tiny leaves at the base of its foliage. If the leaf comes off, the fruit is ripe; if not, the pineapple is not yet ready to eat. Pineapples are most easily peeled with a cleaver. These are heavy and give the leverage needed to make peeling a quick, simple task.

Cut pineapple into 2.5 cm/1 inch cubes. Slice papaya halves. Cut mango flesh into bite-size discs. Combine these fruits in a large bowl and toss gently. Cover and chill in refrigerator for up to 3 hours.

An hour before serving, remove fruit from refrigerator. Peel bananas and slice into fruit bowl. Sprinkle mixture with white wine and rum and toss. Taste for sweetness. If tart, sprinkle lightly with sugar and toss again.

Spoon into an attractive serving dish and serve.

— 6 SERVINGS —

COMMAND PERFORMANCE

M E N U

◆

*S*MOKED MACKEREL
AND AVOCADO GRATIN

◆

*B*EEF FILLET WITH
PEPPER AND PARSLEY
CRUST

◆

*B*UTTERY ONION
SQUARES

◆

*C*HILLED ZABAGLIONE
WITH RASPBERRY
PURÉE

◆

*C*INNAMON STARS

OPPOSITE: BEEF FILLET WITH PEPPER
AND PARSLEY CRUST

Although ramekins are needed for two of the recipes in this menu, the custards can be un-moulded well in advance of mealtime, freeing the ramekins for use with the first course.

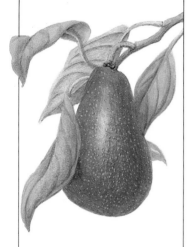

If smoked mackerel is unavailable, substitute fillet of smoked haddock or of smoked cod. In which case, place a 350 to 400 g/12 to 14 oz piece of either in a pan just large enough to hold it comfortably and pour enough boiling water over the fish to cover it. Cover and let steep for 5 to 10 minutes, depending on the thickness of the fish; then drain off the water. Transfer the fish to kitchen paper and pat it to absorb any excess water.

$\mathscr{S}$MOKED MACKEREL AND AVOCADO GRATIN

THE SAUCE FOR THIS DISH CAN BE MADE UP TO A DAY IN ADVANCE, then brought back to a simmer before assembling, and the fish can be skinned and broken into pieces ahead. But the mackerel and all other ingredients should not be combined until just before the ramekins are to be put under the grill.

75	g/2½ oz unsalted butter
40	g/1¼ oz plain flour
600 ml/1 pint milk
350 g/12 oz boneless smoked mackerel
1	large or 2 small avocados, peeled, stoned and diced
	Salt
	Freshly ground pepper
5	tablespoons freshly grated Parmesan cheese

In a heavy, medium-sized saucepan, melt 60 g/2 oz of the butter over low heat. Add flour and stir until smooth. Simmer for 2 minutes, stirring. Pour in the milk and stir over medium-high heat for 4 to 6 minutes, or until the sauce comes to the boil and thickens to the consistency of single cream. Simmer gently, uncovered, for 20 minutes, stirring occasionally.

Lift the skin from the mackerel fillets, scrape away any soft fat that adheres to the flesh, and break the fish into rough half-bite-size chunks.

Preheat the grill.

Remove sauce from the heat, stir in mackerel and avocado and season lightly with salt and pepper. Return saucepan to the heat and warm the mixture for 1 to 2 minutes, or until avocado and fish are heated through. Divide mixture among 8 individual ramekins. Sprinkle about 2 tea-spoons of the Parmesan cheese over the top of each ramekin and set them on a grill pan.

Place under the grill for 1 to 2 minutes, or until cheese is melted and sauce is just starting to bubble around the edges. Serve immediately.

— 8 SERVINGS —

$\mathscr{B}$EEF FILLET WITH PEPPER AND PARSLEY CRUST

THE BEEF CAN BE EATEN ALONE OR SANDWICHED BETWEEN SPLIT AND buttered scone squares to make miniature sandwiches.

1	kg/2 lb joint beef fillet, trimmed
2	teaspoons whole black peppercorns
2	teaspoons whole white peppercorns
2	teaspoons whole dried green peppercorns
2	teaspoons sea salt
60	g/2 oz butter, very soft
60	g/2 oz flat-leaf parsley, chopped

TO SERVE
1 large bunch flat-leaf parsley, stalks removed

Allow beef to come to room temperature before cooking.

Preheat oven to 230° C/450° F/Gas 8.

Wrap black, white and green peppercorns in a tea towel or a double thickness of muslin and crack with a wooden mallet or the bottom of a heavy frying pan. Set aside on a large plate along with the salt. In a small bowl, combine butter and chopped parsley, beat until smooth and rub mixture generously over beef. Roll beef in the crushed peppercorn mixture, coating all sides completely.

Roast beef on a rack in a shallow roasting pan in the centre of oven for 25 to 30 minutes, or until a meat thermometer inserted into the centre registers 54° C/130° F., basting meat every 10 minutes as it cooks. (Meat will be rare.) Remove from the oven and let cool to room temperature, about 1 hour.

Using a very sharp knife, slice meat thinly and arrange overlapping slices in the centre of a large serving platter. Surround meat generously with parsley. Serve at room temperature.

— 8 SERVINGS —

For a different presentation, offer a choice of condiments with the beef: for example, a robust mustard and a piquant, creamy horseradish sauce.

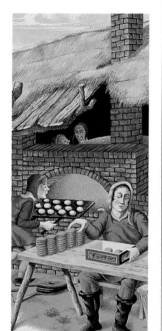

$\mathcal{B}$UTTERY ONION SQUARES

THESE VERY LIGHT SCONES ARE QUICKLY MADE, AND BECAUSE THE dough is cut into squares the re-shaping of scraps that comes with using a round cutter is avoided. Brushing the tops with buttermilk gives them a shine; using melted butter instead leaves the tops just as nicely browned but not shiny.

280 g/10 oz plain flour
1   tablespoon baking powder
½   teaspoon bicarbonate of soda
½   teaspoon salt
165 g/5½ oz butter
2   spring onions, thinly sliced
200 ml/7 fl oz buttermilk

Preheat oven to 220° C/425° F/Gas 7.

Sift flour, baking powder, bicarbonate of soda and salt into a large mixing bowl.

In a small frying pan, melt 15 g/½ oz of the butter over medium-low heat, add spring onions and sauté until softened but not browned, about 3 minutes. Remove from heat and let cool.

Cut remaining butter into small pieces and rub into flour mixture until mixture resembles coarse crumbs. Make a well in the centre of mixture, add spring onions and 175 ml/6 fl oz of the buttermilk, and mix just until a sticky dough forms. Turn dough out on to a lightly floured surface and knead 15 to 20 times. Roll or pat dough into a 1 cm/½ inch thick square. Using a sharp knife, cut into sixteen 5 cm/2 inch squares. Place squares 5 cm/2 inches apart on a baking sheet, brush tops with remaining buttermilk and bake in the centre of oven for 12 to 15 minutes, or until they are well risen and lightly browned on top.

Serve warm with butter.

— MAKES 16 SQUARES —

CINNAMON STARS

THESE VERY CRISP, LIGHTLY SPICED BISCUITS MAKE A LOVELY ACCOMpaniment to a creamy dessert such as zabaglione.

140 g/5 oz plain flour
1½ teaspoons ground cinnamon
　　Pinch salt
125 g/4 oz unsalted butter, softened
110 g/scant 4 oz light brown sugar
1　size 3 egg yolk
2　tablespoons caster sugar

Cinnamon Quill.

Sift flour, cinnamon and salt together on to a sheet of greaseproof paper.

In a large mixing bowl, cream butter and brown sugar together until light and fluffy. Add egg yolk and beat until light. Add flour mixture and blend well. Cover and chill dough for at least 1 hour or overnight.

Preheat oven to 180° C/350° F/Gas 4.

Divide dough in half. On a lightly floured surface, roll out half of dough 3 mm/⅛ inch thick. Using a 6 cm/2½ inch star-shaped biscuit cutter, cut out biscuits and place them 5 cm/2 inches apart on a lightly greased baking sheet. Roll and cut out second half of dough and arrange on baking sheet. Sprinkle biscuits with caster sugar.

Bake in the centre of hot oven for 7 to 8 minutes, or until firm and just beginning to brown around the edges. Transfer to a wire rack and let cool. Store in a tightly covered container.

— MAKES ABOUT 30 BISCUITS —

To turn these star-shaped biscuits into edible decorations for the Christmas tree, carefully work a small hole into one of the points of the baked but still warm biscuits, using a sharp metal skewer. When the biscuits are cool thread a red ribbon through the hole and hang the Cinnamon Star on the tree.

Cinnamomum zeylanicum

Chilled Zabaglione with Raspberry Purée

SMOOTHER THAN A BAKED CUSTARD, BUT LIGHTER THAN A BAVARIAN cream, this moulded dessert can be served with any fruit purée. When serving it as a dinner party dessert, offer whipped cream as an accompaniment as well as the purée.

500 ml/16 fl oz milk
7 g/¼ oz powdered gelatine
1 tablespoon cornflour
5½ tablespoons caster sugar
6 size 3 egg yolks
175 ml/6 fl oz Marsala

PURÉE
175 to 350 g/6 to 12 oz raspberries
Caster sugar

This combination of flavours, turned around, produces another luscious dessert: fresh raspberries with warm zabaglione as a sauce. To serve 4, divide 350 g/12 oz raspberries among 4 individual dishes. In a medium mixing bowl whisk 4 egg yolks with 2 tablespoons caster sugar and 175 ml/6 fl oz Marsala. Just before serving, set the bowl over a saucepan of simmering water and whisk the mixture for about 5 minutes, or until it is light and fluffy. Spoon the zabaglione over the raspberries immediately and serve.

Pour the milk into a small heavy saucepan, bring just to the boil and remove immediately from the heat. Place 4 tablespoons cold water in a small bowl and sprinkle with the gelatine.

In a medium bowl, combine cornflour and sugar, then whisk in the egg yolks until the mixture is smooth. Slowly pour half the hot milk into the egg mixture, whisking constantly. Pour the egg-milk mixture slowly back into the milk remaining in the saucepan and stir over medium heat until the custard thickens and begins to bubble. Stir softened gelatine into the custard until dissolved. Pour the custard into a mixing bowl and let cool for 5 minutes. Stir in the Marsala. Divide mixture among 8 individual ramekins or pour it into a single 1 litre/2 pint bowl or mould. Chill in the refrigerator until set, about 1½ hours for ramekins or 2½ hours for a larger mould.

Purée raspberries in a blender or food processor. Pass purée through a sieve, add sugar to taste and stir until sugar dissolves.

To serve, run a knife carefully around the inside edges of the ramekins and gently turn the custards on to individual dessert plates or a single serving dish. Spoon a little of the raspberry purée around or over the custards decoratively and serve remaining purée separately in a bowl or jug.

— 8 SERVINGS —

LUNCH

LUNCH IN THE OLD DAIRY

MENU

◆

*B*UTTERMILK SQUASH
SOUP

◆

*B*READ SALAD

◆

*W*ALNUT BISCUITS
WITH STILTON

◆

*F*RESH PEARS

OPPOSITE: BUTTERMILK SQUASH SOUP,
WALNUT BISCUITS, STILTON, FRESH
PEARS, AND BREAD SALAD

$\mathcal{B}$READ SALAD

A COLOURFUL ASSORTMENT OF DICED VEGETABLES TOSSED WITH bread cubes to absorb their juices makes a handsome, light main course for lunch. The salad can be made a day before, to the point where the bread is added and refrigerated, but bring the ingredients to room temperature before serving.

For a hotter, more fragrant dressing, 2 to 3 tablespoons Crabtree & Evelyn Olive and Sunflower Oil with Herbs may be used instead of the same amount of olive oil.

3	to 4 ripe plum tomatoes (about 250 g/8 oz)
1	day-old loaf French or Italian bread (about 250 g/8 oz), thickly sliced

DRESSING

6	tablespoons olive oil
2	tablespoons sunflower oil
4	tablespoons red wine vinegar
1	tablespoon finely chopped fresh basil leaves
	Salt
	Freshly ground black pepper

1	small cucumber, seeded and diced
1	small red onion, diced
1	small yellow pepper, cored, seeded and diced
1	tablespoon drained capers
1	small head radicchio, shredded
¼	Cos lettuce, shredded

TO SERVE

10	radicchio leaves
10	Cos lettuce leaves
3	fresh basil leaves

Into a medium saucepan of boiling water, plunge the tomatoes (one at a time) and boil over high heat for 30 seconds. Drain, rinse in cold water and peel. Cut each tomato in half and gently scoop out and discard seeds. Dice tomatoes and place in a large mixing bowl.

Tear bread slices into rough 1 cm/½ inch pieces and add to the mixing bowl.

In another bowl, whisk together the olive oil, sunflower oil, vinegar and basil. Season with salt and pepper. Add the cucumber, onion, yellow pepper and capers to the vinaigrette and toss together well. Let stand for 20 to 30 minutes.

Add the vegetable-vinaigrette mixture to the bread and tomatoes and toss to mix well.

Let stand at room temperature for 30 minutes to 1 hour to allow the bread to absorb juices.

Just before serving, add shredded radicchio and lettuce and toss. To serve, line an attractive salad bowl or serving platter with the whole radicchio and lettuce leaves. Spoon bread salad on to the bed of leaves and garnish with basil leaves.

Serve as an antipasto.

— 4 GENEROUS SERVINGS —

ℬUTTERMILK SQUASH SOUP

THIS SOUP CAN BE MADE AHEAD AND GENTLY REHEATED, BUT DO NOT
let it boil. For a summer version, use nine 10 to 12.5 cm/4 to 5 inch
courgettes in place of the butternut squash. Dice them and cook with the
other vegetables in light oil instead of butter. Substitute 2 teaspoons
finely chopped fresh dill for the rosemary and serve hot or chilled.

45	g/1½ oz butter
1	medium butternut squash (about 750 g/1½ lb), peeled, seeded and cut into cubes
1	medium onion, coarsely chopped
1	medium carrot, coarsely chopped
1	stick of celery, coarsely chopped
500	ml/16 fl oz chicken stock, or 2 chicken stock cubes dissolved in 500 ml/16 fl oz water
1	teaspoon finely chopped fresh rosemary leaves, or ¼ teaspoon dried
250	ml/8 fl oz buttermilk
	Salt
	Freshly ground pepper

TO SERVE
Sprigs fresh rosemary

*Adding the buttermilk
slowly to the hot soup
base, stirring all the
while, prevents curdling.*

Melt butter in a large heavy saucepan. Add squash, onion, carrot and
celery, cover partially and gently cook vegetables over medium-low heat
for 10 minutes, or until softened. Add stock and rosemary. Cover and
simmer over medium heat for about 15 minutes, or until vegetables are
very soft. Remove pan from heat and let mixture cool slightly.

Purée mixture in a food processor or a food mill. Pour into a clean
saucepan, gradually stir in buttermilk and season with salt and pepper.
Cover and cook gently until heated through.

Ladle into shallow soup bowls and garnish each with fresh rosemary.

— 4 SERVINGS (ABOUT 1.25 LITRES/2 PINTS) —

WALNUT BISCUITS

THIS BISCUIT DOUGH CAN BE MIXED, PATTED OUT AND CUT IN ADvance, then frozen on baking sheets. Allow to thaw before baking.

140 g/5 oz plain flour
80 g/2⅔ oz shelled walnuts, finely ground
60 g/2 oz salted butter, cut into pieces and softened

Preheat oven to 200° C/400° F/Gas 6.

Combine flour and walnuts in a food processor or large mixing bowl and process or stir to blend. Add butter and process 10 to 15 seconds or blend briefly by hand until a soft dough forms.

On a well-floured surface, pat dough out 5 mm/¼ inch thick. Using a lightly floured 5 cm/2 inch cookie cutter, cut out dough, and place rounds on a lightly buttered baking sheet. Bake in the centre of oven for 15 minutes, or until biscuits are nicely browned on the bottom. Let cool slightly on the baking sheet. Serve with the Stilton and fresh pears.

— MAKES 16 BISCUITS —

These biscuits are delicious eaten with Stilton (still the king of English cheeses) as well as with fresh pears. Stilton is at its best in the autumn and early winter.

In cooking, stir crumbled Stilton into a celery soup just before serving or melt it over hamburgers and steak during the last few moments under the grill.

CHOWDER LUNCH

MENU

◆

*C*RAB AND SWEETCORN
CHOWDER

◆

*B*ROCCOLI IN LEMON
VINAIGRETTE

◆

*B*ROWN SODA BREAD

◆

*P*OTTED CHEDDAR
CHEESE

◆

*R*ED FRUIT SORBET

OPPOSITE: BROCCOLI IN LEMON
VINAIGRETTE, BROWN SODA BREAD, AND
CRAB AND SWEETCORN CHOWDER

BROCCOLI IN LEMON VINAIGRETTE

THIS SALAD GOES PARTICULARLY WELL WITH GRILLED MEATS.

Lemon is an agreeable seasoning for hot broccoli as well as cold. Add the fresh lemon juice to hot clarified butter according to taste and spike it with a touch of Tabasco, if desired. Pour it into a small warmed jug or sauce boat and serve separately.

1   kg/2 lb fresh broccoli, trimmed and cut into 10 cm/4 inch florets

LEMON VINAIGRETTE
1   tablespoon fresh lemon juice
2   tablespoons white wine vinegar
1   teaspoon Dijon mustard
125 ml/4 fl oz vegetable oil
¼   teaspoon freshly grated lemon zest
½   teaspoon salt
     Pinch freshly ground black pepper
     Tabasco, or other hot pepper sauce, if desired

TO SERVE
½   red onion, thinly sliced
8   thin slices lemon

In a large saucepan of lightly salted boiling water, cook broccoli until crisp-tender, about 3 minutes. Drain and refresh broccoli under cold water. Shake off excess water and drain on kitchen paper. Place on a serving dish, cover tightly with cling film and chill.

In a small bowl, whisk together lemon juice, vinegar and mustard. Whisk in oil. Add lemon zest, salt, and pepper and season with Tabasco, if desired.

Just before serving, toss the broccoli with the vinaigrette and arrange on a platter with the red onion slices. Garnish with lemon slices.

— 4 TO 6 SERVINGS —

Lemon Bonbons

CRAB AND SWEETCORN CHOWDER

LIKE MOST CHOWDERS, THIS DEVELOPS A DEEPER FLAVOUR IF ALLOWED to stand for a few hours or overnight before serving. In this case, make sure that it cools uncovered; otherwise the broth may sour. Reheat the chowder gently before serving.

- 15   g/½ oz butter
- 90   g/3 oz streaky bacon, finely diced
- 1   medium onion, chopped
- 1   bay leaf
- ½   teaspoon dried thyme
- 2   medium potatoes, peeled and diced
- 330 g/11 oz fresh sweetcorn kernels or thawed frozen sweetcorn kernels
- 250 ml/8 fl oz single cream
- 250 ml/8 fl oz milk
- 250 g/8 oz cooked, cleaned white crab meat or lobster meat
- 2   tablespoons dry sherry
-     Salt
-     Freshly ground pepper

TO SERVE
- 1   tablespoon chopped fresh parsley

In a large heavy saucepan, melt the butter and cook bacon over low heat until fat is rendered and meat is crisp, about 15 minutes. Transfer bacon with a slotted spoon to kitchen paper to drain and reserve for garnish.

Add onion to fat remaining in saucepan and cook over medium heat until softened and translucent but not browned, about 5 minutes. Break bay leaf in half and add to pan. Add thyme, potatoes and 350 ml/12 fl oz water. Bring to a simmer over medium heat, then cover, reduce heat to low and simmer for 20 minutes.

Stir in sweetcorn, cream and milk. Bring back to a simmer and cook, uncovered, for 5 minutes. Add crab meat and simmer for 2 to 3 minutes longer, or until potatoes are tender. Stir in sherry. Season with salt and pepper. Ladle into individual serving bowls, garnish each with chopped parsley and the crisp bacon and serve hot.

— 4 TO 6 SERVINGS (ABOUT 1.5 LITRES/2½ PINTS) —

Chowder, a classic of American cooking, is a gift from France. In times past, Breton fishermen made a communal stew from their catch, cooking it in an iron pot, a chaudière, *which gave its name to the dish. The pot and its contents travelled with the fishermen to Newfoundland and then through the eastern reaches of Canada to New England.*

POTTED CHEDDAR CHEESE

Potting is a traditional English method of preserving—for the short term—meat, fish and cheese. With cheese, pieces too dry or small for the cheese board are transformed into a mellow dish. Butter, seasonings and cream or wine are the other basic ingredients. The result tastes of fine cooking, not frugality.

Cheddar or any mild cheese is the obvious candidate for potting, but a blue cheese mixed with butter and brandy is delicious too. Or blend blue and Cheddar cheeses together.

THIS IS A SIMPLE POTTED CHEESE, OF WHICH VARIATIONS ABOUND. White wine may be substituted for Madeira, and the mixture can be flavoured with a generous pinch of cayenne pepper, ¼ teaspoon grated nutmeg or ground mace, 2 to 3 teaspoons of made mustard, or ½ to 1 teaspoon curry powder. For a herb cheese, add 2 tablespoons finely chopped fresh thyme, chives, sage or savory, or 2 teaspoons dried.

250 g/8 oz mature Cheddar cheese, grated
90 g/3 oz unsalted butter
2 tablespoons Madeira or medium-dry sherry

In a food processor, blend the cheese and butter until mixture forms a ball. Add Madeira and process until the mixture is well blended and softened.

Transfer mixture to a small bowl and serve at room temperature surrounded by bread or savoury biscuits.

— 4 TO 6 SERVINGS —

BROWN SODA BREAD

280 g/10 oz plain flour
210 g/7 oz wholemeal flour
1 teaspoon bicarbonate of soda
1 teaspoon baking powder
1 teaspoon salt
60 g/2 oz unsalted butter, cut into pieces
500 ml/16 fl oz buttermilk (see Note)

Preheat oven to 190° C/375° F/Gas 5.

Combine the plain and wholemeal flours, bicarbonate of soda, baking powder and salt in a food processor and pulse with on/off motion to mix. Add butter and process for 15 seconds. With motor running, pour in buttermilk through feed tube and process for 10 seconds, or until a wet but manageable dough forms.

Turn dough out on to a well-floured board and shape lightly into a

20 cm/8 inch round. Cut a deep cross in the centre of the loaf. Bake on a buttered baking sheet in the centre of the oven for 1 hour, or until the loaf sounds hollow when thumped lightly on the bottom. Turn out on to a wire rack and let cool.

Serve warm in thick slices or cold and thinly sliced.

— MAKES 10 TO 12 THICK SLICES —

Note: If buttermilk is not available, in a bowl combine 2 tablespoons vinegar with 500 ml/16 fl oz milk.

$\mathcal{R}$ED FRUIT SORBET

IF FRESH STRAWBERRIES ARE NOT AVAILABLE, SUBSTITUTE 600G/1¼ LB frozen ones in light syrup, omitting the sugar and sugar syrup.

300 g/10 oz fresh strawberries, hulled
600 g/1¼ lb red seedless grapes
200 g/7 oz sugar
2   tablespoons Cognac or brandy

Purée berries and grapes in a food processor.

In a medium saucepan, combine sugar with 500 ml/16 fl oz water and bring to the boil, swirling pan from time to time, until sugar is dissolved. Cook over medium heat for 1 minute. Stir puréed fruit into sugar syrup and cook at a gentle simmer over low heat for 5 minutes.

Strain mixture through a medium-mesh sieve set over a large bowl, pressing firmly with the back of a wooden spoon to extract as much juice and pulp as possible. Discard contents of sieve. Stir Cognac into sorbet and chill in refrigerator for at least 30 minutes.

Pour mixture into container of an ice cream or sorbet machine (sorbetière) and prepare according to manufacturer's instructions. Pack into a container and freeze for at least 3 hours.

— MAKES 1 LITRE/1¾ PINTS —

SOUP AND SANDWICH LUNCH

MENU

◆

*L*EEK AND KALE SOUP

◆

*C*HICKEN PAILLARD
SANDWICHES WITH
WATERCRESS AND
MUSHROOMS

◆

*R*ASPBERRIES WITH
PEACH PURÉE

◆

*C*HOCOLATE WAFERS

OPPOSITE: CHICKEN PAILLARD
SANDWICHES WITH WATERCRESS AND
MUSHROOMS

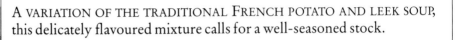

LEEK AND KALE SOUP

A VARIATION OF THE TRADITIONAL FRENCH POTATO AND LEEK SOUP, this delicately flavoured mixture calls for a well-seasoned stock.

45   g/1½ oz butter
1   medium onion, chopped
2   shallots, chopped (optional)
400   g/14 oz leeks (white and light green parts only), thinly sliced
1   clove garlic
250   g/8 oz potatoes, peeled and coarsely chopped
1.25 to 1.5 litres/2 to 2½ pints chicken stock
   Bouquet garni, composed of 1 sprig parsley, 1 bay leaf and 1 sprig each (or ¼ teaspoon dried each) marjoram, thyme and rosemary, tied together in a muslin bag
200   g/7 oz kale, de-ribbed and finely shredded
1   tablespoon finely chopped fresh marjoram leaves, or 1 teaspoon dried
125   ml/4 fl oz double cream
1   to 2 teaspoons fresh lemon juice
   Salt
   Freshly ground pepper

TO SERVE
4   tablespoons finely chopped fresh chives or spring onions

In a large heavy saucepan, melt the butter, add onion, shallots and leeks and simmer, covered, over very low heat for 10 minutes, stirring occasionally to prevent vegetables from browning. Add garlic, potatoes, 1 litre/1¾ pints of the stock and bouquet garni. Cover partially and simmer over medium-low heat for 15 to 20 minutes, or until potatoes are tender. Discard bouquet garni. Let soup cool slightly, then purée in a food processor or blender and return the mixture to the saucepan.

Add kale and marjoram and simmer over medium-low heat for 15 minutes. Stir in cream and simmer 5 minutes longer. Add enough of the remaining stock to dilute mixture to desired consistency. Season to taste with lemon juice, salt and pepper.

Serve hot, sprinkled with chives or spring onions.

— 6 SERVINGS —

Chocolate Wafers

As with other refrigerator biscuits, these can be frozen as an uncooked log of dough and thawed just before baking.

- 140 g/5 oz plain flour
- ½ teaspoon baking powder
- ¼ teaspoon bicarbonate of soda
  Pinch salt
  Pinch freshly ground pepper
- 90 g/3 oz unsalted butter, softened
- 60 g/2 oz light brown sugar
- 50 g/1⅔ oz caster sugar
- 1 size 3 egg yolk
- 1 teaspoon vanilla essence
- 30 g/1 oz plain chocolate, melted (see Note)

Sift flour, baking powder, bicarbonate of soda, salt and pepper on to a sheet of greaseproof waxed paper.

In a large mixing bowl or food processor, cream together butter, brown sugar and caster sugar until mixture is light and fluffy. Add egg yolk and beat until mixture is very well blended. Beat in vanilla essence and chocolate. Add dry ingredients and mix by hand or with an electric mixer at low speed until well blended.

Form dough into a smooth log about 4 cm/1½ inches in diameter. Wrap in greaseproof paper and chill for at least 3 hours or up to 2 days.

Preheat oven to 190° C/375° F/Gas 5.

Using a sharp knife, slice dough 3 mm/⅛ inch thick. Place wafers 4 cm/1½ inches apart on ungreased baking sheets and bake in the centre of oven for 7 to 9 minutes, or until gentle pressure of a fingertip leaves no mark on the surface. Transfer wafers to wire racks and let cool completely. Store tightly covered.

— MAKES ABOUT 36 BISCUITS —

Note: To melt chocolate, soften it in a small saucepan set over a larger saucepan of simmering water.

CHICKEN PAILLARD SANDWICHES WITH WATERCRESS AND MUSHROOMS

A FLAMBOYANT-LOOKING BUT LIGHT MAIN-COURSE SANDWICH, THIS can also be made with 275 g/9 oz trimmed, thinly sliced cultivated mushrooms if wild ones are unavailable.

500 g/1 lb boneless chicken breasts, skinned and cut into 8 thin escalopes Salt Freshly ground pepper	1 bunch watercress, washed, drained and tough stalks removed
25 g/¾ oz unsalted butter	5½ tablespoons mayonnaise
1½ tablespoons olive oil	4 French bread rolls
250 g/8 oz fresh edible wild mushrooms	
1 tablespoon finely chopped shallots	TO SERVE Several sprigs fresh watercress
1 tablespoon tarragon vinegar	
2 tablespoons chicken stock or white wine	
2 or 3 sprigs fresh tarragon, or ¼ teaspoon dried tarragon	

If fresh wild mushrooms are unavailable, use dried ones instead, allowing 45 g/1½ oz dried for 250 g/8 oz fresh.

Rinse the dried mushrooms quickly under cold water to remove any dirt, place them in a small bowl and pour warm water over them to cover. Let them soak for 30 minutes, or until plumped, then drain them in a fine-meshed sieve set over another small bowl. Gently squeeze excess liquid from the mushrooms before adding them to the dish.

Season chicken on both sides with salt and pepper.

In a large frying pan, melt 15 g/½ oz of the butter with 1 tablespoon of the oil over medium-high heat. Add chicken and sauté, in batches if necessary, for 30 to 60 seconds per side, or until lightly browned and cooked through. Remove and keep warm. Do not rinse pan.

In pan, melt remaining butter with remaining oil, add mushrooms and shallots and cook over medium-low heat for about 2 minutes, or until shallots are softened. Season with salt and pepper. Remove mushroom mixture with a slotted spoon and set aside, covered to keep it warm.

Preheat grill.

Add vinegar and stock to the frying pan and deglaze over medium-high heat, scraping up any browned bits. Stir in tarragon and simmer mixture for 10 to 15 seconds. Add watercress and toss over low heat for 5 seconds, just until leaves are coated. Remove watercress with a slotted spoon and set aside. Remove the pan from the heat and stir in the mayonnaise.

Cut rolls in half and place under hot grill until lightly toasted.

To assemble, spread roll halves with the flavoured mayonnaise. Arrange 2 chicken paillards on the bottom half of each roll. Top chicken with mushrooms and watercress. Cover with tops of rolls, or serve open-face style.

Place sandwiches on individual plates, garnish each with watercress sprigs and serve.

— 4 SERVINGS —

ℛASPBERRIES WITH PEACH PURÉE

THIS IS A LIGHTER COMBINATION OF THE FLAVOURS IN ESCOFFIER'S famous Pêche Melba, created for Dame Nellie Melba in 1894. The following recipe is equally delicious served in meringue shells for a more formal meal or arranged around a square of Gingerbread (page 126) to round off an informal supper. The Cardamom Custard Sauce (page 242) or 150 ml/¼ pint double cream, whipped, may be substituted for the *crème fraîche*.

The purée can be made several hours ahead but should be stirred before spooning on to the plates. The raspberry vinegar holds the colour of the peaches, adds a subtle tang and heightens the flavour of the raspberries. Pears may be substituted for the peaches and can simply be peeled without being dipped first in boiling water.

4   medium peaches, peeled and the stones removed
2   to 3 teaspoons raspberry vinegar
2   tablespoons icing sugar, or to taste
250 g/8 oz fresh raspberries
150 ml/¼ pint *crème fraîche*

Purée the peaches in a food processor or a food mill fitted with the finest disc. (There should be about 250 ml/8 fl oz purée.) Add the raspberry vinegar and enough of the icing sugar to balance the taste. Refrigerate until serving time.

Divide the purée among 4 dessert plates, spooning it into a semi-circle. Nestle a quarter of the raspberries beside each serving of purée and pass the *crème fraîche* separately.

— 4 SERVINGS —

To peel peaches: bring a saucepan of water to the boil. Off the heat drop 1 peach gently into the boiling water, leave it for 5 seconds and remove it with a fork. With a paring knife slit the peel, which will slip off easily. Repeat the blanching and peeling procedure with the remaining peaches.

CELEBRATING MAY

MENU

◆

*M*AY WINE COCKTAIL

◆

*T*ROUT WITH TARTARE
STUFFING

◆

*G*RATIN OF ASPARAGUS

◆

*S*ALT-CRUSTED
BREADSTICKS
(PAGE 247)

◆

*R*HUBARB CRUMBLE

OPPOSITE: GRATIN OF ASPARAGUS,
SALT-CRUSTED BREADSTICKS, AND
TROUT WITH TARTARE STUFFING

MAY WINE COCKTAIL

THIS IS A VARIATION ON A TRADITIONAL GERMAN SPRINGTIME DRINK, *Maiwein* or *Maitrank*. At its simplest, it consists of Moselle or Rhine wine with sugar and sweet woodruff. Brandy, Benedictine, strawberries, oranges and even Champagne grace more elaborate versions. If woodruff is unavailable, the combination of spicy white wine and raspberry syrup makes a delicious cocktail on its own.

Sweet woodruff (Galium odoratum) is a shade-loving perennial with tiny white flowers. The delicate young leaves, when bruised, have the aroma of freshly cut hay. Woodruff is a classic flavouring for alcoholic drinks in Europe and can be easily grown in the garden.

| 8 | sprigs tender, sweet woodruff, if available (see Note) |
| 1 | bottle medium-dry German white wine such as Riesling |

TO SERVE
| 8 | teaspoons raspberry syrup or Framboise |
| | Sweet woodruff sprigs, if desired |

Gently bruise woodruff leaves between the fingers and place in the bottle of wine. Recork and let steep in the refrigerator for 8 hours, overnight or up to 2 weeks. Strain through a sieve, discarding woodruff leaves.

At serving time, place about 2 teaspoons of the raspberry syrup in the bottom of each of 4 stemmed hock or white wine glasses. Fill almost to the rim with flavoured wine and stir gently to combine. Float a small sprig of woodruff on surface of each cocktail, if desired.

— 4 SERVINGS —

Note: Use only tender young sprigs of woodruff; old leaves have too strong a flavour.

TROUT WITH TARTARE STUFFING

A SIMPLE, WELL-FLAVOURED STUFFING AND A STRIP OF BACON ADD two complementary tastes and textures to fresh trout. The fish can be stuffed early in the day and refrigerated until cooking time.

4	whole trout (300 to 350 g/10 to 12 oz), cleaned
	Salt
	Freshly ground pepper
	STUFFING
2	teaspoons butter
90	g/3 oz fresh mushrooms, thinly sliced
60	g/2 oz fresh breadcrumbs
125	ml/4 fl oz prepared tartare sauce
2	tablespoons finely chopped fresh parsley
4	long rashers streaky bacon
	TO SERVE
	Parsley sprigs

Wipe trout cavities clean with kitchen paper and sprinkle lightly with salt and pepper.

To make the stuffing, melt the butter in a medium-sized frying pan over high heat. Add mushrooms and sauté for 2 minutes, stirring continually, until mushrooms wilt and soften. Remove mushrooms from the heat with a slotted spoon and stir in breadcrumbs, tartare sauce and chopped parsley. Season with salt and pepper.

Preheat grill or build a medium-hot charcoal fire.

Fill trout cavities with stuffing and secure closure with wooden cocktail sticks. Lay each trout on a slice of bacon, perpendicular to it, wrap ends of bacon around the middle and tie once.

Place trout on a rack in a grill pan or in a barbecue fish holder and cook for about 5 minutes per side, or until the bacon is cooked and the trout flesh becomes opaque.

Arrange trout on a bed of parsley sprigs on a platter or serve on individual plates garnished with parsley sprigs.

— 4 SERVINGS —

With trout—and all fish—freshness is of the essence. Fresh trout glistens, with shiny eyes that are not sunken or dull, resilient flesh, and a fresh, clean smell.

GRATIN OF ASPARAGUS

THIS ASPARAGUS DISH, DELICATELY FLAVOURED WITH GARLIC, HAS A particularly golden gratin topping due to the inclusion of a little corn-meal. The cornmeal also enhances the flavour and crunchy texture of the topping.

750 g/1½ lb thin spears fresh asparagus
175 ml/6 fl oz double cream
1   small clove garlic
2   teaspoons finely chopped shallots
     Salt
     Freshly ground pepper
15   g/½ oz fresh breadcrumbs
1   tablespoon cornmeal
1   tablespoon grated Parmesan cheese
2   teaspoons unsalted butter, cut into small pieces

Snap off and discard the tough ends of the asparagus spears. Cut the tips off about 6 cm/2½ inches from the tip ends and slice the remainder of spears into 1 cm/½ inch pieces.

Bring a large saucepan of lightly salted water to the boil, add the asparagus tips and pieces and boil for 2 minutes. Drain the asparagus and plunge it into a bowl of cold water to stop the cooking and to preserve the colour. Drain well.

Place cream and garlic clove in a small saucepan and simmer over low heat until cream is slightly thickened, about 10 minutes.

Preheat oven to 200° C/400° F/Gas 6.

Sprinkle the shallots evenly over the bottom of a generously buttered 1.5 litre/2½ pint shallow baking dish. Scatter the asparagus pieces evenly over the shallots. Arrange a neat row of asparagus tips, all tips pointing in the same direction, at one end of the dish. Continue to arrange rows of asparagus tips until the dish is filled. Season with salt and pepper.

Discard the garlic clove from the thickened cream and pour the cream over the asparagus. Combine the breadcrumbs, cornmeal and Parmesan cheese and sprinkle the mixture evenly over the asparagus. Dot with the butter. (If more convenient, the casserole can be prepared up to this point in advance and refrigerated for several hours before baking.)

Bake for 5 to 8 minutes (or 15 to 20 minutes if casserole has been refrigerated for several hours before baking), or until heated through. Brown top of casserole under grill for 2 to 3 minutes. Serve hot.

— 4 SERVINGS —

$\mathcal{R}$HUBARB CRUMBLE

THE TARTNESS OF YOUNG RHUBARB SET AGAINST THE BUTTERY, SWEET crumble topping makes this a wonderful fruit pudding. Serve it at room temperature with a jug of double cream or with a good vanilla ice cream. Do not refrigerate before serving as the topping will lose some of its crispness.

750 g/1½ lb fresh rhubarb, sliced
    Caster sugar to taste

    CRUMBLE TOPPING
140 g/5 oz plain flour
5½ tablespoons caster sugar
125 g/4 oz unsalted butter, softened

Preheat oven to 180° C/350° F/Gas 4.

In a 1.5 litre/2½ pint baking dish, about 20 cm/8 inches in diameter, arrange rhubarb in a fairly level layer. Sprinkle sugar evenly over rhubarb.

To make the topping, combine flour, sugar and butter in a bowl and rub ingredients together with the fingertips until the mixture resembles coarse bread crumbs. Sprinkle topping lightly over the rhubarb.

Bake in the centre of the oven for 1 hour, or until a knife inserted into the centre of the fruit pierces the rhubarb easily.

— 4 TO 5 SERVINGS —

TEMPTING FÊTE

MENU

◆

BRAISED HAM GLAZED WITH ORANGE MARMALADE

◆

CRUNCHY FENNEL SLAW

◆

WHOLEMEAL & POTATO CLOVERLEAF ROLLS
(PAGE 248)

◆

VEGETABLES PROVENÇALE

◆

ORANGE FLOWER SANDWICH CAKE

OPPOSITE: BRAISED HAM GLAZED WITH ORANGE MARMALADE

BRAISED HAM GLAZED WITH ORANGE MARMALADE

THIS MAKES A FINE AND PARTICULARLY MOIST CHANGE FROM THE more usual baked ham. Any orange marmalade makes a delicious glaze, and one flavoured with ginger is even better. If the ham has a rind, carefully remove it after braising, leaving a thin layer of fat, and cut a criss-cross diamond pattern into the remaining layer of fat before glazing.

3	tablespoons light vegetable oil
2	carrots, finely chopped
2	sticks of celery, finely chopped
1	1.8 to 2.25 kg/4 to 5 lb precooked, mildly cured ham
250	to 350 ml/8 to 12 fl oz chicken stock
250	to 350 ml/8 to 12 fl oz dry red wine
1	bouquet garni composed of 1 bay leaf, 3 parsley sprigs, 2 thyme sprigs and 1 strip orange zest tied together with kitchen string in muslin
8	to 10 black peppercorns
250	g/8 oz orange marmalade

Preheat the oven to 160° C/325° F/Gas 3.

In a deep heavy flame-proof casserole or baking dish large enough to hold the ham comfortably, heat the oil over high heat until it is hot but not smoking. Add the carrots and celery and cook the vegetables over medium heat, stirring occasionally, until soft but not browned.

Set the ham on the bed of vegetables and add the stock and wine in equal quantities until the liquid reaches halfway up the sides of the ham. Add the bouquet garni and the peppercorns and bring the liquid to a simmer. Cover the casserole with a lid or foil and bake the ham for 1 to 1¼ hours, basting 2 or 3 times with the braising liquid.

Remove the ham from the oven, transfer it to a roasting tin and let it rest at room temperature. Raise the oven temperature to 230° C/450° F/Gas 8.

Spread about half the marmalade over the ham to make a thin layer of glaze and return the ham to the oven for 10 minutes. Spread the ham with another thin layer of marmalade and bake it for 10 minutes more. Let the ham cool and then chill it in the refrigerator before slicing.

— 8 TO 10 SERVINGS —

If serving the ham hot, the cooking liquid makes an excellent sauce. Strain it into a saucepan, discarding the vegetables and seasonings. Taste the liquid to see if the flavour is sufficiently full; if not, boil it rapidly until the sauce becomes more concentrated.

This may be served as a thin sauce; if a slightly thicker consistency is preferred, for every 250 ml/8 fl oz sauce whisk in a mixture of 1 teaspoon cornflour and 1 tablespoon cold water. Bring the sauce to the boil, whisking constantly until it is thickened and the cloudiness of the cornflour has cleared.

CRUNCHY FENNEL SLAW

600 g/1¼ lb green cabbage, finely chopped, reserving
    large outer leaves for garnish
90 g/3 oz fennel bulb, finely shredded
35 g/1¼ oz carrot, grated
30 g/1 oz red onion, thinly sliced

FENNEL SEED DRESSING (SEE NOTE)
1 size 3 egg yolk
4 teaspoons white wine vinegar
½ teaspoon salt
4 tablespoons sunflower oil
4 tablespoons hazelnut oil
125 ml/4 fl oz soured cream
½ teaspoon fennel seed
⅛ teaspoon freshly ground pepper
    Pinch caster sugar

In a large mixing bowl, toss together cabbage, fennel, carrot and onion.

To make dressing, in a food processor blend egg yolk, vinegar and salt with an on-off motion or beat in a bowl with a wire whisk until blended. With processor running, slowly add a little of the oil through the feed tube until mixture starts to thicken. Add remaining oil in a thin, steady stream through feed tube until thoroughly incorporated. If mixing by hand, add oil a few drops at a time, beating constantly with a wire whisk, until mixture starts to thicken. Add remaining oil in a thin, steady stream, beating constantly, until well blended. Add soured cream, fennel seed, pepper and sugar and process or whisk until blended.

Add dressing to shredded vegetables and toss until combined well. Cover and chill slaw for at least 30 minutes, but not more than 3 or 4 hours, before serving. (If dressing is added more than 4 hours ahead, slaw will become watery.)

To serve, line a salad bowl or large serving platter with reserved cabbage leaves and arrange slaw on top.

— 8 TO 10 SERVINGS —

Note: The dressing can be made in advance and stored in a covered container in the refrigerator until tossed with vegetables.

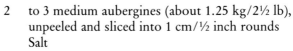EGETABLES PROVENÇALE

AS ONLY A HINT OF GARLIC IS CALLED FOR, GARLIC LOVERS MAY WANT to add 1 to 3 finely chopped garlic cloves to the onion in the last minute of frying. Once assembled, the casserole may be refrigerated for a day or may be frozen.

2	to 3 medium aubergines (about 1.25 kg/2½ lb), unpeeled and sliced into 1 cm/½ inch rounds
	Salt
250	ml/8 fl oz olive oil
6	courgettes (each about 12.5 cm/5 inches long), sliced lengthways into 1 cm/½ inch strips
1	large red pepper, seeds and membranes removed, flesh cut into 1 cm/½ inch wide strips
1	large green pepper, seeds and membranes removed, flesh cut into 1 cm/½ inch wide strips
1	large onion, chopped
	Fresh ground black pepper
3	tablespoons chopped fresh basil, or 2 teaspoons dried
1	clove garlic, smashed
8	fresh plum tomatoes, sliced
125	ml/4 fl oz tomato juice
45	g/1½ oz fresh breadcrumbs
90	g/3 oz Cheddar cheese, grated
30	g/1 oz Parmesan cheese, grated

Put the aubergine slices, sprinkled with salt, in a large colander and let them drain for 30 to 60 minutes.

Preheat the oven to 180° C/350° F/Gas 4.

Spread 2 tablespoons of the oil on the bottom of each of 2 roasting pans. Wipe the salt and moisture from the aubergine slices and lay them, with the courgette strips, in the pans. Sprinkle 1 tablespoon of the remaining oil over the vegetables, cover the pans with foil and roast for an hour, turning the slices after 30 minutes.

Meanwhile, in a frying pan cook the peppers and onion in 4 to 6 tablespoons of the remaining oil with a sprinkling of salt and a few grinds of black pepper over medium heat for about 5 minutes, or until softened. Stir in the basil.

Rub a 3 litre/5 pint baking dish with the garlic clove and lightly oil it. Layer the 2 vegetable mixtures and the tomatoes in the dish. Pour the tomato juice over the vegetables and season, if necessary, with salt and pepper. Mix together the breadcrumbs and cheeses and sprinkle over all. Finally, drizzle 1 tablespoon of the remaining oil over the top.

Bake the casserole, uncovered, for 1 hour, or until heated through, bubbling around the edges and crusty on top.

— 8 TO 10 SERVINGS —

ORANGE FLOWER SANDWICH CAKE

THE CAKE LAYERS MAY BE MADE AHEAD AND FROZEN, THEN THAWED, assembled and iced early on the day of serving. Orange curd can be used to fill the cake in place of the marmalade mixture. Store leftover cake, tightly covered, in a cool place or in the refrigerator.

This cake celebrates the versatile orange. Orange zest, flesh, juice and blossoms contribute different tones of the orange flavour. And not just to sweet foods: dried bitter, or Seville, orange zest lends a special perfume to a bouquet garni, whereas the juice of a sweet, or blood, orange gives a lift to vinaigrettes for avocado and chicken salads.

CAKE
350 g/12 oz plain flour
4 teaspoons baking powder
½ teaspoon salt
250 g/8 oz unsalted butter, softened
400 g/14 oz caster sugar
4 size 3 eggs, at room temperature
1½ tablespoons orange flower water
250 ml/8 fl oz milk, at room temperature
Grated zest of 1 orange

FILLING
325 g/11 oz orange marmalade, at room temperature
325 g/11 oz orange curd
1 teaspoon Grand Marnier or other orange-flavoured liqueur or brandy

TO DECORATE
2 tablespoons icing sugar
Fresh orange flowers and leaves or thinly sliced orange zest

Preheat oven to 180° C/350° F/Gas 4.

Sift flour, baking powder and salt on to a sheet of greaseproof paper.

In a large mixing bowl, cream together butter and sugar until mixture is light and fluffy. Add eggs, one at a time, beating about 2 minutes after each addition. Beat in orange flower water. Alternately add dry ingredients and milk to butter-egg mixture in 3 additions of dry ingredients and 2 of milk, mixing very gently, until batter is just blended. Stir in orange zest.

Butter three 22.5 cm/9 inch sandwich tins, line them with rounds of buttered parchment paper and dust them with flour. Divide the batter among the tins and smooth tops.

Bake for 25 to 30 minutes, or until layers begin to pull away from sides of tins and a skewer inserted in centres comes out clean. Let cool 10

For another version of this opulent dessert, make half the quantity of orange filling. Spread this on the bottom layer. Whip 300 ml/½ pint double cream and fold in 30 g/1 oz grated bitter chocolate; use this for the second filling. Set the third layer on the whipped cream and place a paper doily on top.

Refrigerate until an hour before serving. Just before bringing the cake to the table, sift 2 tablespoons icing sugar over the doily and carefully lift off the doily, leaving a white lacy pattern on the top of the cake.

minutes in tins. Carefully turn cakes out on to wire racks and let cool completely.

Meanwhile, in a small bowl, stir together marmalade, orange curd, and Grand Marnier and set aside.

To assemble cake, place one layer on a cake plate and on it spread half of filling evenly. Add second layer, spread evenly with remaining filling and top with third layer. Sift the icing sugar over the cake and garnish with orange flowers and leaves or with the orange zest.

— 12 SERVINGS —

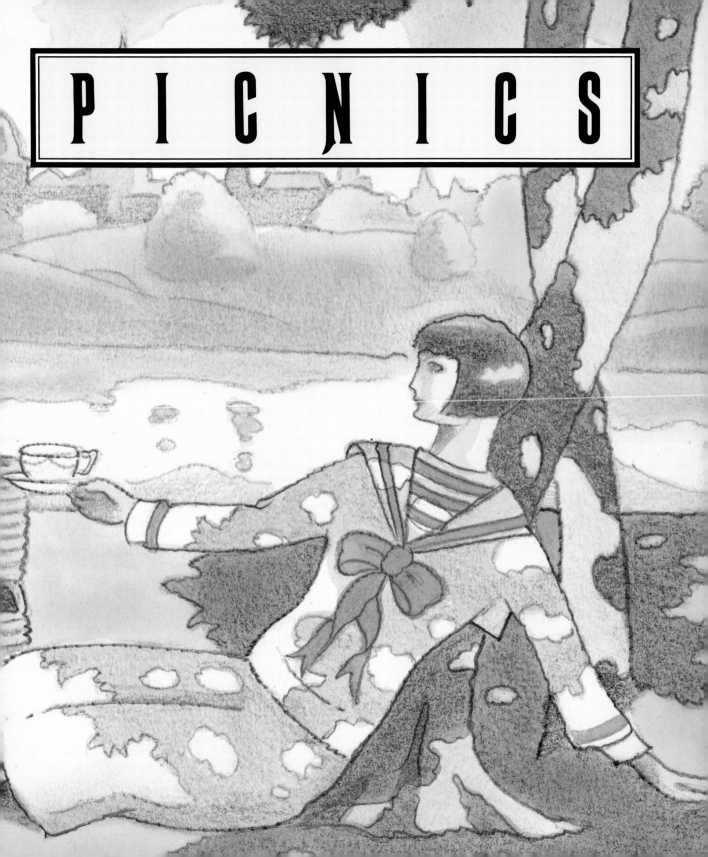

PICNICS

WEATHER PERMITTING...

MENU

◆

*S*ALTED PINE NUTS

◆

*C*OOLING BORSCHT

◆

*C*HICKEN AND MELON SALAD

◆

*L*IGHT HERBED RICE CAKE

◆

*H*ALF MOON PASTRIES

OPPOSITE: COOLING BORSCHT AND
SALTED PINE NUTS

SALTED PINE NUTS

These tiny nuts also give a distinctive texture and delicate nutty flavour to rice, vegetable dishes and stuffings for meats, fish and vegetables.

AFTER TOASTING PINE NUTS, LET THEM STAND FOR AN HOUR TO allow their flavour to develop. Or roast them a day before they are needed and store in an airtight container. They can also be sprinkled, in place of almonds, over chicken salad, trout or lightly steamed mange-touts turned quickly in butter.

    90   g/3 oz pine nuts
    2   teaspoons cold unsalted butter, diced
    1   teaspoon finely ground sea salt

Preheat oven to 150° C/300° F/Gas 2.
    Spread pine nuts out in one layer on a baking sheet. Dot with butter. Roast in oven for 5 minutes. Stir nuts to coat evenly with melted butter. Continue roasting for 15 minutes, or until they are a deep golden, but not dark, brown. Remove from oven, sprinkle with salt and let cool.

— MAKES 90 G/3 OZ —

COOLING BORSCHT

For a hearty hot borscht, remove the bay leaf when the vegetables are softened and purée the soup. Add the grated beetroots, cook the soup until the beetroots are tender, and season with lemon juice. Do not add the cornflour.

THIS BORSCHT, SERVED CHILLED HERE, MAY ALSO BE SERVED HOT, omitting the yogurt and topping each portion instead with a spoonful of soured cream just before serving.

    500 g/1 lb raw beetroot (about 5), peeled
    1   onion, chopped
    1   carrot, chopped
    1   leek, washed and chopped
    1   stick of celery, chopped
    6   peppercorns
    1   bay leaf
    1   tablespoon red wine or sherry vinegar
    2   litres/3½ pints beef stock
    1   tablespoon cornflour
    250 ml/8 fl oz plain yogurt
    2   to 4 tablespoons fresh lemon juice

Coarsely grate 2 beetroots and set aside. Slice remaining beetroots and combine in a large enamel or other non-reactive saucepan with onion, carrot, leek, celery, peppercorns, bay leaf, vinegar and stock. Bring to the boil over high heat, reduce heat to low and simmer, covered, for about 1 hour, or until the beetroots have faded to brownish pink and vegetables are very soft.

Strain liquid into another saucepan, pressing beetroots and vegetables with the back of a spoon to extract as much juice as possible. Discard beetroots and vegetables.

Add reserved grated beetroots to liquid, cover and simmer over low heat for 15 minutes, or until tender.

In a small bowl, blend cornflour with 1 tablespoon cold water. Stir into borscht and bring to the boil, stirring constantly. Remove from heat and let cool. Blend in yogurt and enough lemon juice to add a pleasant tartness. Cover and refrigerate until well chilled.

— 6 SERVINGS —

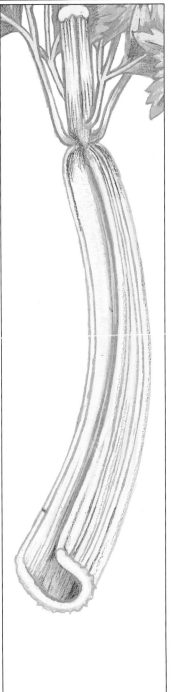

Chicken and Melon Salad

THE DARK MEAT OF CHICKEN THIGHS MARRIES WELL WITH THIS RICHLY flavoured dressing. Meat from a 2 kg/4 lb roast duck may also be used. The chicken (or duck) can be cooked the day before, and the dressing prepared well in advance.

2   kg/4 lb chicken thighs
     Salt
     Freshly ground pepper

DRESSING
3   tablespoons red wine vinegar
1   teaspoon Dijon mustard
1   teaspoon sesame oil
1   teaspoon soy sauce
125 ml/4 fl oz groundnut oil
2   tablespoons chopped mango chutney
¼   teaspoon finely chopped or grated fresh root
     ginger
¼   teaspoon crushed dried chillies
1   garlic clove, smashed
¼   teaspoon salt

TO ASSEMBLE
1   small ripe rock, Ogen or Charentais melon,
     peeled, seeded and cubed
½   large cucumber, peeled, seeded and diced
30   g/1 oz spring onion (white and some green), thinly
     sliced

Preheat oven to 190° C/375° F/Gas 5.

Arrange chicken thighs on a wire rack in a roasting pan. Sprinkle with salt and pepper. Bake in oven for 25 minutes, or until juices run clear when meat is pierced with a knife at its thickest point. Remove from oven and let cool slightly. Remove skin, strip meat from bones and cut meat into cubes. Let chicken cool completely.

To make dressing, combine vinegar, mustard, sesame oil, and soy sauce in a small bowl. Gradually add groundnut oil, whisking constantly until well incorporated. Stir in chutney, root ginger, chilli flakes, garlic and salt. Cover and set aside at room temperature for at least 1 hour to allow flavours to blend.

Combine cooled chicken cubes, melon, cucumber and spring onion in a large bowl and toss. Cover bowl and refrigerate for up to 4 hours.

To assemble, remove garlic clove from dressing, whisk to blend and pour enough over salad to coat ingredients thoroughly. Toss gently, taste for seasoning and arrange on a serving platter.

— 6 SERVINGS —

$\mathcal{L}$IGHT HERBED RICE CAKE

FOR A PICNIC, SERVE THESE CHEESE- AND HERB-FLAVOURED RICE squares warm or at room temperature. They are also delicious eaten hot with a tomato sauce and thin slices of cold rare roast lamb or beef.

200 g/7 oz uncooked medium-grain rice
1 teaspoon salt
60 g/2 oz butter, melted
125 g/4 oz medium Cheddar cheese, grated
2 tablespoons finely chopped onion
2 tablespoons finely chopped fresh dill, or 2 teaspoons dried
4 tablespoons finely chopped fresh parsley
1 size 3 egg, lightly beaten
125 ml/4 fl oz milk
¼ teaspoon Tabasco or other hot pepper sauce
Pinch freshly ground black pepper

Preheat oven to 180° C/350° F/Gas 4.

In a medium saucepan, combine rice, salt and 500 ml/16 fl oz water. Bring to the boil over high heat. Cover tightly, reduce heat to lowest setting and cook for 15 to 18 minutes, or until rice is tender but still lightly firm to the bite. Remove from heat and fluff rice with a fork.

In a large mixing bowl, combine butter, cheese, onion, dill, parsley, egg, milk, Tabasco and black pepper and blend well. Add rice and toss to combine well.

Press mixture evenly into a lightly buttered 20 or 22.5 cm/8 or 9 inch square baking dish. Bake in the centre of oven for 35 to 40 minutes, or until rice is beginning to brown lightly around the edges and become crusty. Remove from oven and let cool for 20 minutes before cutting. Run a small knife around edges of dish and cut rice into 5 cm/2 inch squares.

— 4 TO 6 SERVINGS —

*H*ALF MOON PASTRIES

PASTRY MADE WITH A COMBINATION OF CREAM CHEESE AND BUTTER has a melting texture and delicate flavour. If an assortment of preserves is used, vary the slits on top of pastries or cut slits in the shape of small letters to indicate the flavour of the jam inside. If serving at home, dust pastries lightly with icing sugar just before serving.

140 g/5 oz plain flour
½   teaspoon salt
90   g/3 oz cold cream cheese, cut into small pieces
90   g/3 oz cold unsalted butter, cut into small pieces
about 200 g/7 oz cherry preserve,
     or different flavoured thick fruit preserve or
     marmalade
1   size 3 egg, beaten
2   teaspoons milk or cream

In a large mixing bowl, combine flour and salt. Add cream cheese and butter and rub in with the fingertips until mixture resembles coarse crumbs. Sprinkle with 2 tablespoons iced water and toss with a fork to moisten ingredients. If mixture seems dry, add 1 to 3 more teaspoons water, mixing until dough can be gathered into a ball. Flatten into a disc, wrap with cling film or greaseproof paper and chill for at least 30 minutes.

Preheat oven to 220° C/425° F/Gas 7.

On a lightly floured surface, roll out dough to a thickness of 3 mm/ ⅛ inch. Using a 10 cm/4 inch biscuit cutter or a small plate as a guide, cut dough into circles. Re-roll scraps to make more circles. (There should be 12 to 15.)

Spoon 2 teaspoons of preserve into centre of each pastry round. Brush edge of each with some of the beaten egg. Fold dough over preserve to form half moons. Press edges down firmly with your fingers, then press with the prongs of a fork to seal well. Beat milk into the remaining beaten egg and brush mixture over the tops of the turnovers. Make a small slit in the top of each to allow steam to escape.

Arrange turnovers about 2.5 cm/1 inch apart on an ungreased baking sheet. Bake in the centre of oven for 18 to 20 minutes, or until the pastry is golden brown and crisp. Let turnovers cool on a wire rack.

— MAKES 12 TO 15 PASTRIES —

Individual double-crust mincemeat tartlets are a traditional part of English Christmas feasting, eaten at teatime or at the end of a meal. Use this dough to make them particularly elegant. Shape them into crescent moons for a more generous proportion of mincemeat to pastry.

PUNTING DOWNSTREAM

MENU

◆

PRAWN AND SCALLOP
SALAD

◆

BASIL CORNBREAD

◆

CRUNCHY LEMON
SYRUP CAKE

OPPOSITE: BASIL CORNBREAD, CRUNCHY
LEMON SYRUP CAKE, AND PRAWN AND
SCALLOP SALAD

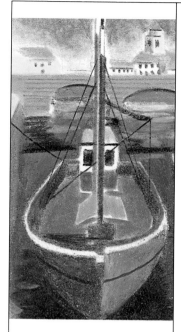

PRAWN AND SCALLOP SALAD

WHEN QUEEN SCALLOPS ARE NOT AVAILABLE, USE ORDINARY LARGE scallops and cut them in quarters before cooking. If lobster is available and affordable, vary this salad by using 500 g/1 lb diced cooked lobster meat in place of prawns and scallops, eliminating the poaching.

DRESSING
4	tablespoons white wine vinegar
½	teaspoon Crabtree & Evelyn Garlic & Parsley Mustard or Dijon mustard
½	teaspoon salt
	Pinch freshly ground black pepper
150	ml/¼ pint vegetable oil
3	tablespoons finely chopped shallots
1	clove garlic, finely chopped
1½	tablespoons finely chopped fresh parsley
1	tablespoon finely chopped fresh chervil, or 1 teaspoon dried

SALAD
175	ml/6 fl oz dry white wine
1	bay leaf
1	clove garlic, split
12	large raw prawns
250	g/8 oz queen scallops
32	mange-touts, stalks and strings removed
250	g/8 oz Cos lettuce, shredded
16	cherry tomatoes, halved
1½	tablespoons finely chopped fresh parsley

TO SERVE
1	lemon, quartered

Alternatively, 'cook' the prawns and scallops in citrus juice for a wonderfully clear taste. In a shallow glass dish, arrange the shellfish in 1 or 2 layers and cover them with fresh lemon and/or lime juice. Season with salt, pepper, garlic slivers and a few onion slices. Cover the mixture with cling film and chill it for several hours or overnight, turning the seafood to ensure that all surfaces lose their raw look and acquire the creaminess of cooked fish. Before serving, drain the seafood on kitchen paper, then dress and arrange it on the salad.

To make dressing, combine vinegar, mustard, salt and pepper in a small bowl. Gradually add oil, whisking constantly until well incorporated. Add shallots, garlic, parsley and chervil and blend well. Taste and correct seasoning, if necessary.

In a medium-sized, non-reactive saucepan, combine wine, bay leaf, garlic and 250 ml/8 fl oz water. Bring to a simmer over medium heat and simmer for 5 minutes. Meanwhile, remove shells from prawns, leaving tails on, and devein them. Simmer prawns gently in poaching liquid for about 2 minutes, or just until they turn bright pink. Using a slotted spoon, transfer prawns immediately to a small bowl, let cool slightly, then spoon 3 tablespoons dressing over them. Set aside to cool completely. Add scallops to poaching liquid and simmer for 30 seconds, or just until they turn white and opaque. Transfer immediately to a small plate and let cool (but without adding any dressing). When cool, cover prawns and scallops and refrigerate separately.

Bring a large saucepan of water to the boil. Add mange-touts and boil for 30 seconds. Turn into a colander and rinse under cold water to stop cooking and set colour. Spread on a layer of kitchen paper to drain. Refrigerate until needed.

To assemble, add scallops to bowl with the prawns. Add remaining dressing and toss to coat well. On a large serving platter or, for a picnic, in individual plastic containers with covers, make a bed of shredded lettuce. Scatter mange-touts on top. Remove prawn and scallop mixture from dressing with a slotted spoon, reserving dressing, and spoon seafood over mange-touts. Garnish with tomatoes and parsley.

Just before serving, drizzle reserved dressing over salad and garnish with lemon quarters.

— 4 SERVINGS —

Should you have access to scallops in the shell, serve the coral sections as well, treating them just as you would the creamy flesh.

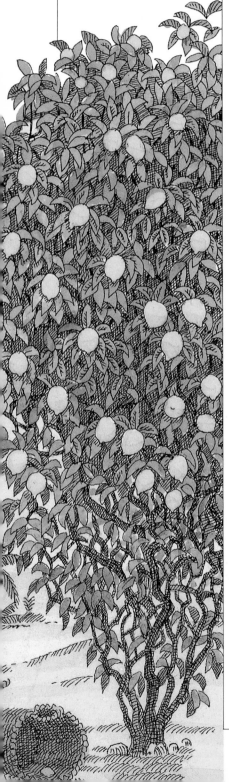

BASIL CORNBREAD

THIS BREAD MAY BE MADE EARLY IN THE DAY FOR AN EVENING MEAL, or in the evening for lunch the next day. Other herbs may be substituted for basil.

60	g/2 oz unsalted butter
100	g/3½ oz plain flour
85	g/scant 3 oz cornmeal
2	teaspoons baking powder
½	teaspoon salt
⅛	teaspoon freshly ground pepper
1	size 3 egg
150	ml/¼ pint milk
2	tablespoons finely chopped fresh basil, or 2 teaspoons dried

TO SERVE
Unsalted butter, softened

Preheat oven to 200° C/400° F/Gas 6.

In a small saucepan, melt butter over very low heat. Remove from heat and let cool completely.

Sift flour, cornmeal, baking powder, salt and pepper into a mixing bowl. In a small bowl, beat egg lightly, add milk, basil and cooled butter and stir into the flour mixture all at once until just blended.

Turn batter into a greased 20 cm/8 inch square baking tin and smooth top with a spatula. Bake in centre of oven for 15 to 18 minutes, or until light golden and beginning to pull away from edges. Let cool completely. Serve cut into 5 cm/2 inch squares, split horizontally and buttered.

— MAKES SIXTEEN 5 CM/2 INCH SQUARES —

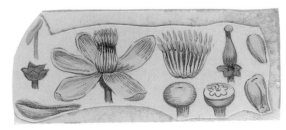

CRUNCHY LEMON SYRUP CAKE

SERVE THIS CAKE WHILE IT'S STILL SLIGHTLY WARM, TOPPED WITH
unsweetened whipped cream. It keeps for two to three days if kept in an
airtight container.

    140 g/5 oz plain flour
    ¾   teaspoon baking powder
    ¼   teaspoon bicarbonate of soda
         Pinch salt
    60   g/2 oz unsalted butter, softened
    135 g/4½ oz caster sugar
    1   size 3 egg
    5½   tablespoons buttermilk or sour milk
    1   tablespoon grated lemon zest

         SYRUP
    100 g/3½ oz sugar
    5½   tablespoons fresh lemon juice

Preheat oven to 180° C/350° F/Gas 4.

Sift together flour, baking powder, bicarbonate of soda and salt and
set aside.

In a large mixing bowl, cream together butter and sugar with an
electric mixer or by hand until light and fluffy. Add egg and beat at high
speed for 1 minute or vigorously by hand. Alternately add buttermilk
and flour mixture in 3 additions, with mixer at low speed or stirring by
hand. Stir in lemon zest.

Turn batter into a buttered and floured 20 cm/8 inch springform cake
tin, smoothing the top of batter with a spatula. Bake in the centre of oven
for 30 to 35 minutes, or until a skewer inserted into centre of cake comes
out clean.

Before cake is finished baking, in a saucepan combine sugar and
lemon juice over low heat to make a syrup. Spoon syrup evenly over cake
as it comes from the oven. Tip and rotate cake tin gently so that the
syrup is distributed evenly over the surface of the cake.

Set cake, in its tin, on a wire rack to cool.

— 6 TO 8 SERVINGS —

*This cake is also excellent
when cooled, carefully
sliced horizontally to
form two layers and
filled with one of the
Crabtree & Evelyn
'fruit only' conserves.*

SPORTING AFTERNOON

MENU

◆

*W*ILD MUSHROOM
BROTH

◆

*S*PRING CHICKENS
WITH HONEY AND
GINGER

◆

*P*ASTA CONFETTI
SALAD

◆

*G*RAPE TARTLETS
WITH ALMOND PASTRY

OPPOSITE: WILD MUSHROOM BROTH,
SPRING CHICKENS WITH HONEY AND
GINGER, PASTA CONFETTI SALAD,
AND GRAPE TARTLETS WITH
ALMOND PASTRY

WILD MUSHROOM BROTH

THIS MAKES A BRACING THERMOS FLASK SOUP FOR A HIKE ON A COLD winter day. The better the quality of the beef stock, the more flavourful the soup. Any edible dried wild mushrooms can be used, but ceps (also called funghi porcini) are among the most flavourful. If fresh herbs are not available for the bouquet garni, use ¼ teaspoon each of dried herbs.

1.5 litres/2½ pints beef stock
45 g/1½ oz dried ceps or other edible dried wild mushrooms
1 bouquet garni composed of 1 small bay leaf and 1 fresh sprig each parsley, thyme, marjoram and rosemary, all tied together with string
3 tablespoons Madeira or medium sherry
Salt
Freshly ground pepper

In a medium-sized saucepan, warm 500 ml/16 fl oz of the stock over medium heat. Place mushrooms, rinsed, in a bowl, add warm stock and let soak for 30 minutes.

Pour reconstituted mushrooms and their liquid back into the saucepan, being careful to hold back any dirt or sand that has settled at the bottom of the bowl. Add remaining stock and bouquet garni and bring to a simmer over medium-low heat. Cover and simmer for 30 minutes.

Remove from heat and strain mixture through a muslin-lined sieve. When mushrooms are cool enough to handle, squeeze them in the muslin to extract as much liquid as possible and discard mushrooms. Stir Madeira into stock, season with salt and pepper if necessary (if stock is made from a cube, extra salt may not be desirable) and serve hot.

— 4 SERVINGS —

To make a basic beef stock, in a stockpot or large heavy saucepan combine 250 g/8 oz stewing beef and 500 g/ 1 lb beef bones, sawn into pieces by the butcher if necessary, with 1 onion, 1 leek, 1 carrot, ¼ small turnip, and a bouquet garni. Season with salt and pepper and a grating of nutmeg and add 2 litres/3½ pints cold water.

Bring the water to the boil, skim off any froth that rises to the surface and simmer the mixture for 1 to 1½ hours. Strain through a fine sieve and let cool.

Refrigerate until any fat solidifies on the surface. Remove the fat with a spoon before using the stock. The stock may be frozen.

*S*PRING CHICKENS WITH HONEY & GINGER

THIS SWEET, SPICY GLAZE IS AN EXCELLENT COMPLEMENT TO THE MILD flavours of these small chickens and to the pasta and vegetable salad. Serve the birds hot or at room temperature, and for easier handling on a picnic, cut each in half.

2	spring chickens
1	tablespoon olive oil
	Salt
	Freshly ground pepper
	GLAZE
5½	tablespoons Crabtree & Evelyn Honey & Ginger Sauce
1	tablespoon dry white wine
1	tablespoon white wine vinegar
1	teaspoon Dijon mustard

Preheat oven to 200° C/400° F/Gas 6.

Remove giblets from birds and reserve for another use. Rinse birds inside and out and pat dry. Using a large, heavy knife or cleaver, split birds in half through breastbones. Lay each bird flat and cut the meat away from the backbone, discarding backbones or reserving them with the giblets for a stock.

Brush chicken halves with oil and season lightly with salt and pepper. Arrange them, skin sides down, on a rack in a shallow roasting pan. Place pan in centre of oven, reduce heat to 180° C/350° F/Gas 4 and roast for 25 minutes.

Meanwhile, combine Honey & Ginger Sauce, wine, vinegar and mustard in a small saucepan. Bring to the boil over medium-high heat, reduce heat to medium-low and simmer for 2 minutes.

Remove chickens from oven and brush generously with warm glaze. Turn halves skin sides up, brush skin generously with glaze and return them to oven to bake for 30 minutes more, basting after 15 minutes with any remaining glaze and pan drippings. Chickens are cooked when juices run clear if thigh meat is pierced at its thickest point with a knife.

— 4 SERVINGS —

The same honeyed piquancy can be given to cold chicken by mixing 2 to 4 tablespoons Crabtree & Evelyn Honey & Ginger Sauce into 250 ml/8 fl oz mayonnaise and sharpening the mixture with a squeeze of lemon. This is also a perfect dressing for a fruit and cottage cheese salad.

GRAPE TARTLETS WITH ALMOND PASTRY

TAKE THESE TO A PICNIC IN THE TINS THEY WERE BAKED IN TO PREVENT crushing. Assemble them not more than 6 hours before serving time. For a single 25 cm/10 inch tart, bake the pastry case for 15 minutes with the foil in and a further 20 to 30 minutes empty.

ALMOND PASTRY
30 g/1 oz blanched almonds
210 g/7½ oz plain flour
¼ teaspoon salt
40 g/1⅓ oz brown sugar
125 g/4 oz cold unsalted butter, cut into small pieces
1 cold size 3 egg
½ teaspoon vanilla essence
¼ teaspoon grated lemon zest

GLAZE
250 g/8 oz apricot preserve
3 tablespoons sherry

TO ASSEMBLE
350 g/12 oz grapes, preferably an assortment of 2 or 3 colours, halved and, if necessary, pipped
30 g/1 oz slivered blanched or unblanched almonds, lightly toasted

This rich nutty crust is a perfect pastry shell for spur-of-the-moment desserts, especially if the pastry is frozen uncooked in the pie tins, then thawed and cooked when needed. Fill with good-quality coffee ice cream and serve with Crabtree & Evelyn Honey & Ginger Sauce or with raspberry ice cream topped with Crabtree & Evelyn Blueberry Fruit Only Conserve.

Finely grind almonds in a food processor with on/off motion, or crush with a rolling pin until as finely ground as possible. Add flour, salt and brown sugar to processor and blend, or combine ground almonds, flour, salt and brown sugar in a bowl and stir to blend. Add butter and process or work with the fingertips until mixture resembles coarse crumbs.

In a small bowl beat egg lightly. Stir in the vanilla essence and lemon zest. With processor on, add egg mixture to dough through feed tube and process until dough forms, or add to mixing bowl, stirring constantly, and stir until dough forms. Pat dough into a ball, wrap in cling film, and chill in refrigerator for at least 30 minutes.

Remove dough from refrigerator and divide into 8 equal pieces. Press each piece into a lightly buttered 7.5 to 8.5 cm/3 to 3½ inch tartlet tin, preferably with removable rim, patting into an even layer. (The dough

will soften as you work with it.) Chill tartlet shells in freezer for at least 30 minutes before baking.

Preheat oven to 200° C/400° F/Gas 6.

Remove tartlet shells from freezer, line each with a square of foil and fill with dried beans to prevent dough from puffing during baking. Bake blind on baking sheet in centre of oven for 10 minutes. Remove foil with beans, reduce oven temperature to 180° C/350° F/Gas 4 and continue baking for 15 to 20 minutes, or until pastry is a rich golden brown. Let tartlet shells cool in tins for 10 minutes. Then carefully remove tartlet shells from tins and place on wire racks to cool completely.

To prepare glaze, combine preserve and sherry in a small saucepan and warm over medium heat, stirring, until preserve is melted. Sieve.

To assemble tarts, brush glaze on the bottom of each tartlet shell. Arrange grapes, cut sides down, in a decorative pattern, alternating colours, in the bottom of each pastry shell. Brush remaining glaze, reheating it if necessary, over grapes and edges of tartlets.

Sprinkle toasted almonds over tartlets before glaze sets. Serve at room temperature.

— MAKES 8 TARTLETS —

Open fruit tartlets or large tarts are among the prettiest summer desserts. For a strawberry or raspberry tart made with this pastry, make a confectioners' custard based on the Cardamom Custard Sauce on page 242, but beat 30 g/1 oz plain flour into the egg yolk and sugar mixture and omit the cardamom. When the cream has been added, bring the custard to a simmer, then lower the heat and cook it, stirring, for 5 to 7 minutes. Add vanilla, let the mixture cool and chill it, covered, until needed. Assemble the tartlets or tart by spreading the confectioners' custard evenly over the fully baked almond pastry. Arrange hulled strawberries or raspberries in concentric circles, stalk ends down, over the custard. Melt 150 g/5 oz redcurrant jelly with 1 teaspoon lemon juice and brush the glaze gently over the fruit.

PASTA CONFETTI SALAD

THIS IS A COLOURFUL SALAD THAT CAN BE MADE WITH OTHER COM-
binations of diced raw and blanched vegetables. To serve the salad at a
picnic, place the bowl or container of salad in the centre of a platter
surrounded with the chicory and radicchio leaves, so that everyone can
fill the leaves with salad and eat them with their fingers.

315 g/10½ oz uncooked orzo (rice-shaped pasta)
Salt

DRESSING
3   tablespoons white wine vinegar
1   teaspoon Dijon mustard
6   tablespoons olive oil

40 g/1⅓ oz carrots, finely chopped
1   plum tomato, seeded and finely chopped
50 g/1⅔ oz green pepper, finely chopped
40 g/1⅓ oz celery, finely chopped
75 g/2½ oz red onion, finely chopped
5   tablespoons finely chopped fresh parsley
    Freshly ground black pepper
1   to 2 heads chicory, leaves separated
1   to 2 heads radicchio, leaves separated

*Pasta salads are light but
nourishing warm-
weather dishes, and the
mixture of vegetables,
meats and fish can be a
matter of choice. For an
attractive effect, cut the
meats and vegetables
used approximately the
same size and shape as
the chosen pasta.*

Bring a large saucepan of water to the boil over high heat. Add orzo and 1
tablespoon salt and boil for about 8 minutes, or until pasta is tender but
still slightly firm. Turn orzo into a sieve, rinse under cold water to stop
cooking and drain well.

In a small bowl, combine vinegar and mustard, then whisk in oil.
Bring a small saucepan of water to the boil over high heat, add carrots
and blanch for 2 minutes. Drain in a colander.

In a large bowl, combine orzo, carrots, tomato, green pepper, celery,
onion, and parsley. Add dressing, season with salt and pepper and toss
to combine well. Serve with the chicory and radicchio.

— 4 TO 6 SERVINGS —

SUMMER'S TEA

MENU

◆

GINGERBREAD

◆

CARDAMOM TOAST

◆

SALLY LUNN
(PAGE 245)

◆

ALMOND TUILES

◆

CHOCOLATE-PECAN BREAD

◆

CHINA TEA AND INDIA TEA

OPPOSITE: ALMOND TUILES, ENGLISH
GINGERBREAD AND SALLY LUNN

GINGERBREAD

MANY GINGERBREADS MUST MATURE FOR SEVERAL DAYS OR A WEEK TO achieve a rich, dark flavour and moistness. This recipe gives the traditional deep flavour but has a lighter texture and can be made as little as one day ahead. It also makes an excellent dessert, cut into larger pieces and served warm with whipped cream.

Ginger in its varied forms is versatile enough to contribute to every course of the meal, and so it is worth keeping the fresh, preserved and ground root as staples in the kitchen. Root ginger can also be potted, to become a large indoor plant with an exotic flower and an exquisitely sweet scent.

20 TEA BAGS

ASSAM

net wt 50 g 1.8 OZ

350 g/12 oz plain flour
1½ teaspoons ground ginger
1 teaspoon ground cinnamon
½ teaspoon ground cloves
¼ teaspoon salt
125 g/4 oz butter
110 g/3¾ oz dark brown sugar
125 ml/4 fl oz (165 g/5½ oz) molasses
125 ml/4 fl oz (165 g/5½ oz) treacle
1 teaspoon grated lemon zest
1 tablespoon freshly grated root ginger
2 size 3 eggs, beaten
2 teaspoons bicarbonate of soda
250 ml/8 fl oz boiling water
3 tablespoons icing sugar

Preheat the oven to 180° C/350° F/Gas 4.

In a large mixing bowl, sift the flour, ginger, cinnamon, cloves and salt together and set aside.

In a small heavy saucepan, heat the butter, brown sugar, molasses and treacle over low heat, stirring, until butter is melted and sugar dissolves. Remove from the heat, cool slightly and stir in lemon zest and root ginger.

Make a well in the centre of dry ingredients and pour in the butter mixture and the eggs. Beat with a wooden spoon until smooth and well blended. In a small bowl, combine bicarbonate of soda and boiling water and stir until dissolved. Pour over batter and stir gently to mix.

Pour batter into a 22.5 cm/9 inch square buttered and floured baking tin and bake in the centre of the oven for 35 to 40 minutes, or until a skewer inserted into the centre comes out clean. Let cake cool in the tin. Dust the top with icing sugar before cutting.

— MAKES 20 PIECES —

$\mathcal{C}$ARDAMOM TOAST

IF MAKING A LARGER QUANTITY, PUT THE SUGARED TRIANGLES OF toast in a very low oven while preparing the remaining pieces. Serve them warm, as they are, or with orange curd.

2	tablespoons caster sugar
½	teaspoon ground cardamom
4	slices firm white bread
	Unsalted butter, softened

Combine sugar and cardamom on a small plate and mix well.

Toast bread slices on both sides and butter both sides well. Cut each slice into 4 triangles. Gently press triangles into the cardamom sugar, coating both sides lightly. Arrange on a platter and serve warm.

— MAKES 16 TOAST TRIANGLES —

Serve these in a basket or warmed shallow dish lined with a cloth napkin to keep the toast warm and help retain the sweet spicy aroma that is released when the napkin is opened at the table.

ALMOND TUILES

THESE CLASSIC BISCUITS ARE SHAPED TO RESEMBLE THE TILES (*TUILES*) on French rooftops. Bake only one batch at a time, as speed is of the essence when removing and shaping the cookies. They may, of course, simply be cooled flat on racks. But don't be afraid to try shaping them; it's a simple procedure that gives an impressive result.

2	size 3 egg whites
100	g/3½ oz caster sugar
	Pinch salt
½	teaspoon vanilla essence
½	teaspoon almond essence
1½	tablespoons dark rum
55	g/scant 2 oz plain flour
60	g/2 oz unsalted butter, melted and cooled
45	g/1½ oz blanched almonds, finely chopped

DECORATION

30   g/1 oz unblanched flaked almonds

EXTRA JAM
PEACH
PRESERVE
and
AMARETTO
with
ALMONDS

Preheat oven to 200° C/400° F/Gas 6. Have ready a clean broom handle for shaping biscuits.

In a mixing bowl, whisk the egg whites with the sugar, salt, vanilla and almond essences and rum until well blended. Stir in the flour and butter until smooth. Then add the chopped almonds. The batter should be very thin.

Drop the batter by teaspoonful on to a large, well-buttered baking sheet, spacing them about 7.5 cm/3 inches apart and baking only about 9 biscuits at a time. With a small spatula, spread the batter evenly into very thin 6 cm/2½ inch circles. Sprinkle each with a few of the flaked almonds.

Bake in the centre of the oven for 5 to 6 minutes, or until the edges are golden. Lay the broom handle across the backs of two chairs to give a rail for shaping the biscuits. Remove biscuits from the oven and, working quickly, lift them from the baking sheet with a fish slice and drape them over the broom handle, curving the edges downward. (If the biscuits become too cool to remove with ease from baking sheet, return them to the oven for about 30 seconds to soften.) Let biscuits cool on the broom handle.

Bake remaining biscuits in the same manner, re-buttering baking sheet between batches.

— MAKES ABOUT 36 BISCUITS —

CHOCOLATE-PECAN BREAD

SERVE THIS BREAD IN THIN SLICES ARRANGED ON A SERVING DISH OR AS a whole loaf on a bread board, sliced as it is needed. Or serve with Cardamom Custard Sauce (page 242) poured around each slice on individual plates or served separately in a sauceboat.

90 g/3 oz plain chocolate	TO SERVE
1 tablespoon instant espresso powder	Icing sugar
250 ml/8 fl oz boiling water	
210 g/7½ oz plain flour	
2 teaspoons baking powder	
¼ teaspoon salt	
125 g/4 oz unsalted butter, softened	
250 g/8 oz caster sugar	
2 size 3 eggs	
1½ teaspoons vanilla essence	
60 g/2 oz shelled pecan nuts, coarsely chopped	

Preheat oven to 180° C/350° F/Gas 4.

Break or chop chocolate into small pieces and heat in the top of a double boiler over simmering water until melted. Set aside to cool completely. In a small bowl, dissolve espresso powder in the boiling water and set aside to cool. Sift flour, baking powder and salt on to a sheet of greaseproof paper and set aside.

Combine butter and sugar in a large mixing bowl and beat with an electric mixer or whisk until light and fluffy. Add eggs, one at a time, beating well after each addition, and beat in vanilla essence. Add chocolate and beat mixture on low speed, if using a mixer, until well blended. Stir in half the espresso mixture and half the flour mixture and blend well. Stir in remaining espresso mixture and remaining flour mixture and stir until blended. Stir in pecans.

Spoon batter into a 10 × 21 cm/4 × 8½ inch buttered and floured loaf tin. Tap tin firmly to remove air pockets. Bake in the centre of oven for 1 hour and 10 minutes, or until the top springs back when pressed lightly and a skewer inserted in the centre comes out clean. Let cool for 10 minutes. Turn out on to a wire rack and let cool completely. Store in cling film or an airtight container. Just before serving, sprinkle bread with icing sugar.

— MAKES 12 TO 14 THIN SLICES —

For picnics, sandwich vanilla, chocolate, coffee or orange icing between two slices of the pecan bread to make a dessert that is delicious and easier to transport than an iced cake.

SMASHING SERVICE

MENU

◆

*W*ATERCRESS
SANDWICHES

◆

*R*ADISH FLOWER
SANDWICHES

◆

*R*ASPBERRIES AND
BLACKBERRIES WITH
RICOTTA CREAM

◆

*C*HOCOLATE
SHORTBREAD

◆

*V*ICTORIA SPONGE

◆

*I*CED HERBAL TEA WITH
GERANIUM SUGAR

◆

*I*CED SPICED COFFEE

OPPOSITE: ICED HERBAL TEA WITH
GERANIUM SUGAR, WATERCRESS
SANDWICHES AND RADISH FLOWER
SANDWICHES

WATERCRESS SANDWICHES

THE WATERCRESS BUTTER THAT IS PART OF THIS RECIPE CAN BE MADE IN advance and frozen.

16 thin slices of white bread
32 small watercress sprigs plus extra watercress for
    decoration
    WATERCRESS BUTTER
125 g/4 oz unsalted butter, softened
90 g/3 oz watercress leaves
1   teaspoon fresh lemon juice
¼   teaspoon freshly ground black pepper
    Pinch cayenne

To make the watercress butter, in a food processor blend the butter, watercress leaves, lemon juice, black pepper and cayenne until the mixture is very smooth. Let the mixture stand for about 30 minutes at room temperature (or chill it but bring it back to room temperature before using).

Spread each slice of bread with about 1½ teaspoons of the watercress butter, and cut 4 rounds from each slice with a 4 cm/1½ inch round or fluted biscuit or canapé cutter. Arrange a watercress sprig on half the rounds, leaving a bit extending over the edge of each, and invert the remaining rounds on top to complete the sandwiches. Serve the sandwiches on a tray decorated with the extra watercress sprigs.

— MAKES 32 TEA SANDWICHES —

Although the watercress we buy is cultivated, the plant grows wild in streams in Britain. Wild watercress should be used only if you are certain that the water where it grows is pure and that no animals, such as grazing sheep or cattle, drink from any part of the stream.

Watercress is usually kept fresh by standing the sprigs in a bowl of water, like a bouquet of flowers, in the refrigerator. It will stay crisp and green longer, though, if the bunch is turned upside-down in the water, so that the leaves are submerged and the stalks extend above the surface.

ℛADISH FLOWER SANDWICHES

125 g/4 oz unsalted butter, softened
1   tablespoon finely chopped fresh chives
1   tablespoon finely chopped flat-leaf parsley
1   tablespoon finely chopped radish
    Salt
8   thin slices firm white bread, crusts removed

TO DECORATE
12 small radishes, very thinly sliced
    Fresh chive blades
    Fresh parsley sprigs
    Whole radishes for flowers (optional)

In a small bowl, combine butter and finely chopped chives, parsley and radish. Season with salt and beat until blended. Spread each bread slice with about 1 tablespoon herb-radish butter. Cut each slice into 4 neat squares.

To decorate, place 2 radish slices, slightly overlapping, on each square. Place a chive blade at the bottom of each radish slice to form the stalk for the flower, and place a sprig of parsley at the base of each chive blade to form a leaf.

Arrange on a platter, garnish platter with additional parsley sprigs and carved radish flowers, if desired, and serve. If not serving immediately, cover lightly and chill. Bring back to room temperature before serving.

— MAKES 32 TEA SANDWICHES —

The herbed radish butter can also be spread on wholemeal bread to add piquancy to roast beef, lamb or fresh salmon sandwiches.

RASPBERRIES AND BLACKBERRIES WITH RICOTTA CREAM

This combination can also be used to fill individual tartlets: shortly before serving, put a layer of the ricotta cream into each tartlet shell and arrange the fruit on top.

PURÉED AND FLAVOURED RICOTTA MAKES A DELICIOUS AND UNUSUAL accompaniment to any juicy fruits.

250 g/8 oz raspberries
300 g/10 oz blackberries
450 g/15 oz ricotta cheese
30 g/1 oz icing sugar
3   tablespoons Amaretto or Grand Marnier

Combine berries in a shallow serving dish.

Drain any excess liquid off ricotta. Purée in a food processor until smooth, add icing sugar and Amaretto and blend well. Spoon into a pretty serving dish and chill.

Serve berries and ricotta cream for guests to scoop spoonfuls of each, side by side, on to dessert plates.

— 8 SERVINGS —

134

CHOCOLATE SHORTBREAD

THIS SHORTBREAD MAY BE CUT INTO MANY SHAPES BUT IS PAR-
ticularly decorative cut out as hearts. The uncooked dough may be
frozen and thawed just before needed.

140 g/5 oz plain flour
45 g/1½ oz unsweetened cocoa powder
60 g/2 oz icing sugar
⅛ teaspoon salt
125 g/4 oz cold unsalted butter, cut into small pieces
1 size 3 egg yolk
1 teaspoon vanilla essence
Caster sugar

Combine flour, cocoa powder, icing sugar and salt in a food processor or
large mixing bowl and process or stir briefly to blend. Add butter and
process about 30 seconds or rub in lightly with the fingertips until
mixture resembles coarse crumbs. Add egg yolk and vanilla essence and
process or stir until a smooth dough forms. Pat dough into a flattened
ball, wrap in cling film, and chill for at least 45 minutes.
   Preheat oven to 160° C/325° F/Gas 3.
   On a lightly floured surface, roll out the dough about 5 mm/¼ inch
thick. Using a heart-shaped, scallop-edged or other fancy biscuit cutter,
2.5 to 5 cm/1 to 2 inches in diameter, cut out shapes and place them
2.5 cm/1 inch apart on lightly greased baking sheets. Sprinkle biscuits
with caster sugar and bake in oven for 15 to 18 minutes, or until firm but
not browned around the edges. Transfer biscuits to a wire rack and let
them cool. Cooled biscuits may be stored in an airtight container.

— MAKES 25 TO 30 BISCUITS —

Shortbread has been a favourite sweet pastry in Scotland for centuries and was once included in several rites of passage there. In some areas a disc of the rich biscuit would have been broken over a bride's head at her wedding, and a piece sewn into the hem of a baby's christening gown, each as a symbol of hope for happiness and prosperity.

$\mathscr{V}$ICTORIA SPONGE

THIS SPONGE CAKE, A VERY SIMPLE, OLD-FASHIONED CAKE, IS A GREAT British favourite. Be sure to use a high-quality jam for the centre. The cake will keep for a couple of days but is at its best fresh. If baked in advance, freeze the sponges as soon as possible, then thaw and fill them only a few hours before serving.

175 g/6 oz butter, softened
200 g/7 oz caster sugar
3   size 3 eggs
280 g/10 oz plain flour
4   teaspoons baking powder
250 g/8 oz strawberry or raspberry jam
2   tablespoons icing sugar

Preheat the oven to 180° C/350° F/Gas 4. Butter and flour two 20 cm/ 8 inch sandwich tins.

In a food processor, cream the butter with the caster sugar for 1 minute. With the motor running add the eggs, 1 at a time, processing for a further 5 seconds after each addition. Sift the flour and baking powder into the bowl of the food processor and pulse the mixture in short bursts several times to fold the dry ingredients into the butter mixture without overbeating it. The mixture will be quite stiff.

Divide the mixture between the 2 tins, gently smoothing the tops, and bake the cakes for 25 to 30 minutes, or until they spring back when lightly touched in the centre. Let the cakes cool in the tins on racks for 10 minutes and then turn the sponges out of the tins on to the racks to finish cooling.

To fill, spread 1 of the sponges with the jam and top it with the second sponge. Sift the icing sugar over the top just before serving.

— SERVES 8 TO 10 —

ℐCED HERBAL TEA WITH GERANIUM SUGAR

ROSE AND LEMON GERANIUMS ARE PARTICULARLY SUITABLE FOR flavouring sugar and tea. Geranium tisane can be made by steeping scented geranium leaves (1 or 2 leaves per cup of hot water) with the tea.

2	to 3 scented geranium leaves	2	litres/3½ pints herb tea
100	g/3½ oz caster sugar		Ice cubes

In a small bowl, bury geranium leaves in the sugar, cover the bowl and let stand for 3 days.

Brew tea as usual and let steep to desired strength. Allow to cool. Pour into a jug filled with ice. Add geranium sugar as desired to flavour tea.

— MAKES 2 LITRES/3½ PINTS —

ℐCED SPICED COFFEE

A STRONG BREW OF COFFEE IS NEEDED FOR THIS RECIPE, AS THE ICE cubes will melt and dilute it.

2	litres/3½ pints fresh strong coffee	TO SERVE
1	stick cinnamon	Ice cubes
½	teaspoon grated nutmeg	Double cream
10	pods cardamom, bruised	
	Caster sugar	

Pour the freshly brewed hot coffee into a heatproof glass container. Add cinnamon, nutmeg and cardamom and let cool. Cover and refrigerate for at least 4 hours. Strain coffee through a sieve and discard spices. Add sugar to taste, stirring until it is dissolved.

To serve, pour coffee into tall glasses filled with ice. Pass a jug of double cream separately.

— MAKES 2 LITRES/3½ PINTS —

To keep ice cubes from diluting drinks, freeze tea, coffee and fruit juices in ice cube trays and use these flavoured cubes to cool the appropriate beverages.

CROQUET AND CUCUMBER SANDWICHES

MENU

◆

*C*UCUMBER AND MINT
SANDWICHES

◆

*C*URRANT CREAM
SCONES

◆

*C*OCOA MERINGUE
KISSES

◆

*S*EED CAKE

◆

*W*ALNUT TARTLETS
WITH FRUIT CURDS

◆

*J*ASMINE TEA

◆

*G*UNPOWDER TEA

OPPOSITE: WALNUT TARTLETS WITH
FRUIT CURDS AND JASMINE TEA

*C*UCUMBER AND MINT SANDWICHES

A REFRESHING VARIATION ON ONE OF ENGLAND'S MOST TRADITIONAL tea sandwiches, thinly sliced cucumber on good buttered bread. The crusts are always removed.

1	small cucumber	
32	small fresh mint leaves	
125	g/4 oz unsalted butter, softened	
1	teaspoon grated orange zest	
8	thin slices firm white bread, crusts removed	
8	thin slices firm wholemeal bread, crusts removed	

TO SERVE
Fresh mint sprigs
Thin orange slices

Peel the cucumber, halve lengthways, and slice crossways as thinly as possible. In a small bowl, combine mint leaves, butter and orange zest and stir until creamy and blended.

Spread each slice of white bread with about 1½ teaspoons of the butter mixture. Arrange several slices of cucumber on each slice and top with the wholemeal bread. Cut each sandwich into quarters to make 4 squares or triangles.

To serve, arrange sandwiches on a platter, alternating white and wholemeal sides of sandwiches, and garnish with mint sprigs and orange slices.

— MAKES 32 TEA SANDWICHES —

*C*URRANT CREAM SCONES

SCONES MAY BE MADE EARLIER IN THE DAY AND REHEATED IN A 200° C/400° F/Gas 6 oven for 5 minutes before serving. They may also be frozen as soon as they have cooled after baking.

280	g/10 oz plain flour	90	g/3 oz butter, cut into 10 pieces
2	teaspoons baking powder	125	g/4 oz currants
2	tablespoons caster sugar	2	size 3 eggs, well beaten
½	teaspoon salt	140	ml/4½ fl oz double cream

Preheat oven to 220° C/425° F/Gas 7.

Sift flour, baking powder, 1 tablespoon of the sugar and the salt into a mixing bowl. Add butter and rub into flour mixture with the fingertips until mixture resembles coarse crumbs. Add currants and toss.

Keep a supply of mint butter in the freezer to use when fresh mint is out of season.

To make it, soften 250 g/8 oz unsalted butter in a food processor and add 3 to 4 handfuls of clean, dry mint leaves. Process until smooth. Roll the butter into a log (or logs), wrap it in parchment paper, twisting the ends tightly, and freeze it. Slice the frozen mint butter into rounds as needed.

Make a well in flour mixture and add eggs and 125 ml/4 fl oz of the cream. Mix with a wooden spoon until dough begins to clump together, then knead in the bowl for about 30 seconds; do not overwork dough.

Turn dough out on to a lightly floured surface and halve. Form each half into a ball and flatten to form a circle about 2 cm/¾ inch thick and 12.5 cm/5 inches in diameter. Cut each circle into 8 pie-shaped wedges. Place wedges about 2.5 cm/1 inch apart on a lightly buttered baking sheet. Brush tops with remaining cream and sprinkle lightly with remaining sugar. Bake in the centre of oven for 12 to 15 minutes, or until lightly browned.

Serve warm with raspberry or blackcurrant conserve.

— MAKES 16 SCONES —

Cocoa Meringue Kisses

3	size 3 egg whites
150	g/5 oz caster sugar
4	teaspoons unsweetened cocoa powder
90	g/3 oz plain chocolate

Preheat oven to 105° C/225° F/Gas ¼. Line 2 large baking sheets with parchment paper or butter and flour them lightly.

Beat egg whites in a bowl with an electric mixer at medium speed until they are very foamy and almost to the stage when soft peaks form. Add 100 g/3½ oz of the sugar, 1 tablespoon at a time, beating at high speed after each addition, until a stiff, glossy meringue forms.

In a small bowl, sift together the cocoa powder and remaining sugar. Then sift this mixture over the meringue. Using a large spatula, gently but thoroughly fold the cocoa mixture into the meringue.

Spoon cocoa meringue into a piping bag fitted with a star tube. Pipe 2.5 cm/1 inch rosettes about 2.5 cm/1 inch apart on baking sheets, lifting tip of bag to form small points on the kisses.

Bake meringue kisses in the centre of the oven for about 2 hours, or until the bottoms are dry. Turn oven off and let kisses cool, or transfer them to wire racks to cool.

Meanwhile, gently melt chocolate in a small saucepan over very low heat. When meringues are cooled, dip the top of each kiss into the chocolate and place the kisses on a wire rack to dry.

— MAKES ABOUT 60 KISSES —

Fresh caraway leaves have a mild, dill taste and can be chopped and sprinkled over soups, salads and vegetables.

20 TEA BAGS

CEYLON BROKEN ORANGE PEKOE

net wt 50 g 1.8 OZ

*S*EED CAKE

THIS WONDERFULLY OLD-FASHIONED CAKE KEEPS FRESH IN AN AIR-tight container for several days and also freezes well. It looks handsome served unsliced on a cake stand or can be cut into thin pieces and arranged on a plate.

185 g/6½ oz plain flour
1 teaspoon baking powder
250 g/8 oz unsalted butter, softened
250 g/8 oz plus 2 tablespoons caster sugar
4 size 3 eggs, separated
3 tablespoons whisky
3 tablespoons caraway seeds

TO SERVE
Icing sugar

Preheat oven to 180° C/350° F/Gas 4.

Sift flour and baking powder together on to a sheet of greaseproof paper. In a large mixing bowl, beat butter with 250 g/8 oz of the caster sugar until mixture is light and fluffy. Add egg yolks and whisky and continue beating until smooth.

Gradually add flour mixture and caraway seeds to egg-butter mixture and continue beating until smooth.

In a separate bowl, beat egg whites until soft peaks form. Sprinkle in remaining 2 tablespoons caster sugar and beat until whites are stiff but not dry.

Stir about one third of the meringue into cake batter to lighten it. Gently fold in remaining meringue. Batter will remain quite stiff.

Spoon batter into a generously buttered 20 cm/8 inch springform cake tin with funnel base, lined on bottom with buttered parchment or greaseproof paper, and smooth the top. Bake in the centre of oven for 50 to 55 minutes, or until cake pulls away from sides of tin and a skewer inserted in centre comes out clean. Let cool in the tin for 10 minutes. Turn out on to a wire rack and let cool completely.

Just before serving, sprinkle generously with icing sugar.

— 10 TO 12 SERVINGS —

*W*ALNUT TARTLETS WITH FRUIT CURDS

THERE ARE SEVERAL SIZES AND SHAPES OF MOULDS AVAILABLE FOR making tiny, bite-size tartlets. When these small pastry shells are filled with different curds, in varying shades of yellow, the effect is very attractive. The dough can be made in advance and frozen.

140 g/5 oz plain flour
20 g/⅔ oz ground walnuts
½ teaspoon salt
75 g/2½ oz cold unsalted butter, cut into 8 pieces
300 ml/½ pint fruit curds, preferably of different
flavours such as lemon and orange
TO SERVE
30 g/1 oz shelled walnuts, finely chopped

Combine flour, ground nuts and salt in a mixing bowl or the bowl of a food processor. Add butter and rub in by hand or process briefly until mixture resembles coarse crumbs. Sprinkle with 2 tablespoons iced water and toss with a fork or pulse quickly in processor. Add additional water by teaspoonsful, if needed, until dough is moist enough to hold together. Gather into a ball, flatten into a circle and wrap in cling film. Chill in the refrigerator for 45 minutes.

Preheat oven to 230° C/450° F/Gas 8.

On a lightly floured surface, roll out dough about 3 mm/⅛ inch thick. Cut dough to fit eighteen 4 to 5 cm/1½ to 2 inch tartlet moulds. Ease dough into the moulds and press gently into corners and sides. Trim edges and prick surfaces with a fork. Chill tartlets on a baking sheet for about 20 minutes.

Bake tartlet shells in the centre of oven for 8 to 10 minutes, or until lightly coloured, and let cool slightly in moulds. Carefully invert tartlet moulds and let shells cool completely on a wire rack.

An hour or so before serving, spoon 1 to 2 teaspoons fruit curd into each pastry shell. Sprinkle the top of each with a few chopped walnuts.

— MAKES 18 TARTLETS —

English Country
Lemon
CURD
Made from
WHOLE EGGS
lemon juice,
Sugar & Butter.
Made in England

ENGLISH FARMHOUSE TEA

MENU

◆

*H*AM

◆

*A*N ASSORTMENT OF
STUFFED EGGS

◆

*C*OTTAGE LOAF

◆

*P*OTTED SALMON

◆

*W*HOLEMEAL SCONES

◆

*R*ICH CHOCOLATE
SQUARES

◆

*C*HEDDAR CHEESE

◆

*A*PPLE AND
RAISIN PIE

◆

*D*ARJEELING TEA

◆

*E*ARL GREY TEA

OPPOSITE: HAM, APPLE AND RAISIN PIE,
CHEDDAR CHEESE, COTTAGE LOAF;
WHOLEMEAL SCONES, HARD-BOILED
EGGS AND TINY TOMATOES (NO RECIPE),
POTTED SALMON AND RICH CHOCOLATE
SQUARES

AN ASSORTMENT OF STUFFED EGGS

THE VARIETY OF FILLINGS FOR THESE EGGS PRODUCES A COLOURFUL platter for any buffet. The eggs may be stuffed early in the day, arranged on the platter, loosely covered and refrigerated.

For delicious egg mayonnaise sandwiches, season chopped hard-boiled eggs with any of the filling combinations and make up on wholemeal or black bread.

24 size 5 eggs
1 large bunch fresh parsley

HAM AND WATERCRESS FILLING
60 g/2 oz cooked ham, finely chopped, plus 6 tiny thin triangles cooked ham for garnish
1½ tablespoons finely chopped watercress leaves
2 drops Tabasco or other hot pepper sauce
1 teaspoon Dijon mustard
4 tablespoons mayonnaise, or to taste
  Salt
  Freshly ground black pepper

DILL AND PARSLEY FILLING
1 tablespoon chopped fresh dill, or 1 teaspoon dried
2 tablespoons finely chopped fresh parsley
½ teaspoon Worcestershire sauce
2 tablespoons soured cream
2 tablespoons mayonnaise, or to taste
  Salt
  Freshly ground pepper
6 small sprigs fresh dill, or 6 flat-leaf parsley leaves

TOMATO AND HORSERADISH FILLING
2 teaspoons tomato paste
2 teaspoons prepared horseradish
4 tablespoons mayonnaise, or to taste
  Salt
  Freshly ground pepper
6 5 mm/¼ inch strips tomato

CURRY AND SHALLOT FILLING
1 teaspoon finely chopped shallot
1 teaspoon curry powder
2 tablespoons soured cream
2 tablespoons mayonnaise, or to taste
  Salt
  Coarsely ground pepper

Place eggs in a large saucepan and add enough cold water to cover. Bring to the boil, covered, over medium-high heat, remove from heat and let stand, covered, for about 20 minutes. Drain eggs, rinse well under cold water and peel. Let cool completely.

Discard stalks from parsley. Arrange bed of parsley sprigs on a large platter and chill in the refrigerator while preparing fillings.

To prepare ham and watercress filling, cut 6 of the eggs in half lengthways and carefully remove yolks. Set whites aside. Place yolks in a small mixing bowl, add chopped ham, watercress, Tabasco, mustard and mayonnaise and mash with a fork until blended and smooth. (Add more mayonnaise if needed to make a smooth paste.) Season lightly with salt and pepper and blend. Spoon filling into a piping bag fitted with a star tube and pipe into the hollows of the whites. Garnish each egg with a triangle of ham. Chill, covered.

To prepare dill and parsley filling, cut 6 of the remaining eggs in half lengthways and carefully remove yolks. Set whites aside. Place yolks in a small mixing bowl, add dill, parsley, Worcestershire sauce, soured cream and mayonnaise and mash with a fork until blended and smooth. (Add more mayonnaise if needed to make a smooth paste.) Season lightly with salt and pepper and blend. Spoon filling into a piping bag fitted with a star tube and pipe into the hollows of the whites. Garnish each egg with a dill sprig or parsley leaf. Chill, covered.

To make tomato and horseradish filling, cut 6 of the remaining eggs in half lengthways and carefully remove yolks. Set whites aside. Place yolks in a small mixing bowl, add tomato paste, horseradish and mayonnaise and mash with a fork until blended and smooth. (Add more mayonnaise if needed to make a smooth paste.) Season lightly with salt and pepper and blend. Spoon filling into a piping bag fitted with a star tube and pipe into the hollows of the whites. Garnish each egg with a strip of tomato. Chill, covered.

To make curry and shallot filling, cut remaining 6 eggs in half lengthways and carefully remove yolks. Set whites aside. Place yolks in a small mixing bowl, add shallot, curry powder, soured cream and mayonnaise and mash with a fork until blended and smooth. (Add more mayonnaise if needed to make a smooth paste.) Season lightly with salt and pepper and blend. Spoon filling into a piping bag fitted with a star tube and pipe into the hollows of the whites. Garnish each egg with a generous grinding of coarse pepper. Chill.

To serve, arrange eggs on the bed of parsley.

— MAKES 48 STUFFED EGGS —

To ensure that the eggs will not crack while boiling, add 2 tablespoons vinegar or salt to the water. Peeling the eggs as soon as they are cool enough to handle makes the whites come away from the shells more easily, and eggs that are several days old peel better than do freshly laid ones.

COTTAGE LOAF

THIS COUNTRY LOAF IS TRADITIONALLY SHAPED IN THE FORM OF A large bun with a knob on top. The dough is easy to make and can be shaped and baked in smaller rolls as well.

about 400 g/14 oz plain flour
1   teaspoon salt
½   teaspoon caster sugar
7   g/¼ oz easy-blend dried yeast
150 ml/¼ pint milk
15   g/½ oz butter

In a large mixing bowl or the bowl of a heavy-duty (tabletop) mixer, combine 280 g/10 oz of the flour with the salt, sugar and yeast.

In a small saucepan, combine milk, butter and 125 ml/4 fl oz water and warm over low heat until butter is melted and the liquid feels hot. Pour liquid into dry ingredients and stir with a wooden spoon to make a coarse dough.

Knead by hand for about 8 minutes, adding as much additional flour as is needed to make a smooth, elastic dough.

Turn dough into a large buttered bowl, turning it to coat all sides. Cover bowl loosely with a damp tea towel and set aside to rise in a warm place for about 45 minutes, or until dough is double in bulk. Knock back dough, knead for about 2 minutes and cover and set aside for 30 minutes more, or until double in bulk again.

Knock back dough. Break off about one-quarter of the dough, shape into a small ball and set aside. Shape remaining dough into a large ball and place in the middle of a buttered baking sheet. Place smaller ball on top of the large ball and insert forefinger down through the centre of both balls until finger touches the baking sheet. Let rise for 30 minutes. Meanwhile, preheat oven to 230° C/450° F/Gas 8.

Bake loaf in the centre of oven for 10 minutes. Reduce heat to 190° C/375° F/Gas 5 and bake for 25 to 30 minutes longer, or until the top is golden brown and the loaf sounds hollow when thumped lightly on the bottom. Let cool on a wire rack.

— MAKES 1 LOAF —

This shape can also be used for individual rolls by dividing the dough into 18 equal pieces and forming tiny cottage loaves from each. Bake these at 220° C/425° F/ Gas 7 for about 20 minutes.

$\mathcal{P}$OTTED SALMON

SPREAD THIS MIXTURE ON SCONES, SLICES OF COTTAGE LOAF OR ON toast at teatime. It should be chilled for several hours, but take it from the refrigerator about an hour before serving to allow it to soften to a spreading consistency.

250	ml/8 fl oz dry white wine
1	bay leaf
	Pinch grated nutmeg
	Salt
6	peppercorns
500	g/1 lb fillet of salmon, preferably cut from the tail
125	g/4 oz unsalted butter
2	teaspoons chopped fresh dill, or ½ teaspoon dried
	Freshly ground pepper
	Fresh dill or parsley sprigs

In a small, non-reactive saucepan just large enough to hold the salmon, combine wine, bay leaf, nutmeg, ¼ teaspoon salt and peppercorns. Bring to a simmer and cook for 5 minutes. Add salmon and a tablespoon or so water, or enough for liquid to just cover the fish. Bring to a simmer over medium heat, reduce heat to low and poach for 8 to 10 minutes, or until the fish just loses its translucency. Transfer salmon with a fish slice to a plate and let it cool. Discard the bay leaf and peppercorns and simmer poaching liquid over medium heat until it is reduced to about 2 tablespoons. Set aside.

In a small saucepan, melt 30 g/1 oz of the butter over low heat, skimming off any foam that rises to the top, and set aside to allow milky solids to settle in the bottom.

Remove and discard skin, any small bones and very dark meat from the salmon. Flake fish into the bowl of a food processor. Cut remaining butter into pieces and add to the food processor, along with the dill and poaching liquid. Process with short on/off pulses in order to retain some of the salmon's texture. Season with salt and pepper.

Pack salmon mixture into a crock and smooth the top with a spatula. Lay small sprigs of dill or parsley on top and spoon a thin layer of the clarified butter over the top, being careful to use only the clear liquid, or clarified, butter and avoiding solids. Refrigerate for several hours.

— MAKES ABOUT 500 ML/16 FL OZ —

Potted Salmon, served from the crock or—for more formal meals—in individual ramekins, also makes a fine first course at lunch or dinner. Serve it with strips of warm toast and wedges of lemon. Slightly more clarified butter may be needed to cover the salmon if it is potted in individual dishes.

WHOLEMEAL SCONES

EAT THESE SCONES WARM FROM THE OVEN, SPREAD WITH POTTED ﹀
Salmon (page 149) or an assortment of good jams.

240 g/8 oz wholemeal flour
2½ teaspoons baking powder
½ teaspoon salt
90 g/3 oz cold unsalted butter, cut into 10 pieces
1 size 3 egg
125 ml/4 fl oz milk

Preheat oven to 220° C/425° C/Gas 7.

Sift flour, baking powder and salt into a large bowl, adding any flakes of bran that don't pass through the sieve into the bowl. Add butter and rub it into the flour mixture with the fingertips until the mixture has a grainy texture.

In a small bowl, combine egg and milk and beat together lightly. Make a well in the centre of flour mixture, pour in egg mixture and stir with a wooden spoon until a dough begins to form. Knead dough in the bowl about 15 times, or until it is just smooth.

Turn dough out on to a lightly floured surface and knead 3 to 4 times,

Some cooks are convinced that the extra lightness of their scones results from rubbing the butter into the flour while lifting the ingredients into the air above the bowl and letting them fall—thus introducing more air into the mixture.

then form into a circle about 2 cm/¾ inch thick. Transfer dough to a lightly buttered baking sheet. Using a sharp knife, make a deep cut across the round without slicing all the way through to the baking sheet. Make a second cut at right angles to the first to form 4 quarters. Then mark each quarter into 3 equal wedges to form 12 wedge-shaped scones. Bake in the centre of the oven for 15 to 18 minutes, or until lightly browned.

— MAKES 12 SCONES —

$\mathcal{R}$ICH CHOCOLATE SQUARES

SERVE THESE MOIST, FLAVOURFUL SQUARES PLAIN OR, FOR THE TRUE chocolate addict, ice them with chocolate icing.

125 g/4 oz unsalted butter	1 teaspoon vanilla essence
125 g/4 oz unsweetened chocolate	140 g/5 oz plain flour
4 size 3 eggs	
Pinch salt	TO SERVE
300 g/10 oz caster sugar	Icing sugar

Preheat oven to 180° C/350° F/Gas 4.

In a medium saucepan or in the top of a double boiler, melt butter and chocolate over low heat or simmering water. Remove from the heat and let cool to lukewarm.

Meanwhile, beat eggs and salt in a mixing bowl with an electric mixer for about 2 minutes, or until mixture is light and double in volume. If using a whisk, place bowl over a pan of simmering water. Gradually add sugar, beating constantly. Beat in the vanilla essence. Gradually add the chocolate mixture, beating on low speed. Sift the flour over the mixture and stir with a wooden spoon just until flour is incorporated and no white specks remain.

Turn batter into a buttered 22.5 cm/9 inch square baking tin. Bake in the centre of oven for 30 minutes, or until a shiny crust forms and edges pull away from the tin. Centre should still be moist when tested with a skewer.

Let cool in the tin on a wire rack. Cut into 36 squares, dust with icing sugar and arrange on a platter to serve.

— MAKES 36 SMALL SQUARES —

While these scones are best eaten within a few hours of baking, they freeze well. Reheat by placing them, still frozen, in a 150° C/300° F/ Gas 2 oven for about 10 minutes.

151

Apple and Raisin Pie

PASTRY
350 g/12½ oz plain flour
2 teaspoons caster sugar
½ teaspoon salt
175 g/6 oz cold unsalted butter, cut into pieces
30 g/1 oz cold lard, cut into pieces

FILLING
6 firm tart apples, such as Granny Smith
125 g/4 oz raisins
165 g/5½ oz brown sugar
¼ teaspoon grated nutmeg
½ teaspoon grated lemon zest
½ teaspoon grated orange zest
1 tablespoon fresh lemon juice
1 teaspoon vanilla essence
1 tablespoon plain flour
30 g/1 oz butter, cut into pieces

This filling can also be used as the heart of a winter apple crumble. Mix the ingredients together, put them into a 1.5 litre/2½ pint oven-proof dish and top with a crumble of 125 g/4 oz crushed rolled oats lightly mixed with 90 g/3 oz melted butter and 45 g/1½ oz light brown sugar. Bake at 180° C/350° F/Gas 4 for about 1 hour, or until the juices bubble up around the edges of the topping and the fruit is softened.

To make pastry, combine flour, sugar and salt in the bowl of a food processor and pulse with on/off motion to mix. Add butter and lard and pulse until pieces of fat are the size of broad beans. Add 5½ tablespoons iced water through the feed tube, pulsing with on/off motion until dough begins to clump together. If necessary, add additional iced water by teaspoons until dough forms. Turn dough out on to a lightly floured surface and form into 2 circles, one slightly larger than the other. Wrap the smaller one in cling film and chill. Roll remaining dough out into a 25 cm/10 inch round and fit it into a 22.5 cm/9 inch pie or flan tin. (Do not trim edge.) Cover with polythene and chill for at least 30 minutes.

Preheat oven to 190° C/375° F/Gas 5.

Peel, core and thinly slice apples. In a mixing bowl, toss them with the raisins, brown sugar, nutmeg, zests, lemon juice, vanilla essence and flour, turn mixture into the pastry shell, and dot the top with butter.

Roll out remaining dough into a 23.5 cm/9½ inch round and place it over filling. Press pastry edges firmly together and trim. Crimp edges with the fingertips or the prongs of a fork to seal and then cut slashes in the top crust to allow steam to escape. Bake in the centre of oven for 45 to 55 minutes, or until the crust is golden and the filling bubbly.

— MAKES ONE 22.5 CM/9 INCH PIE —

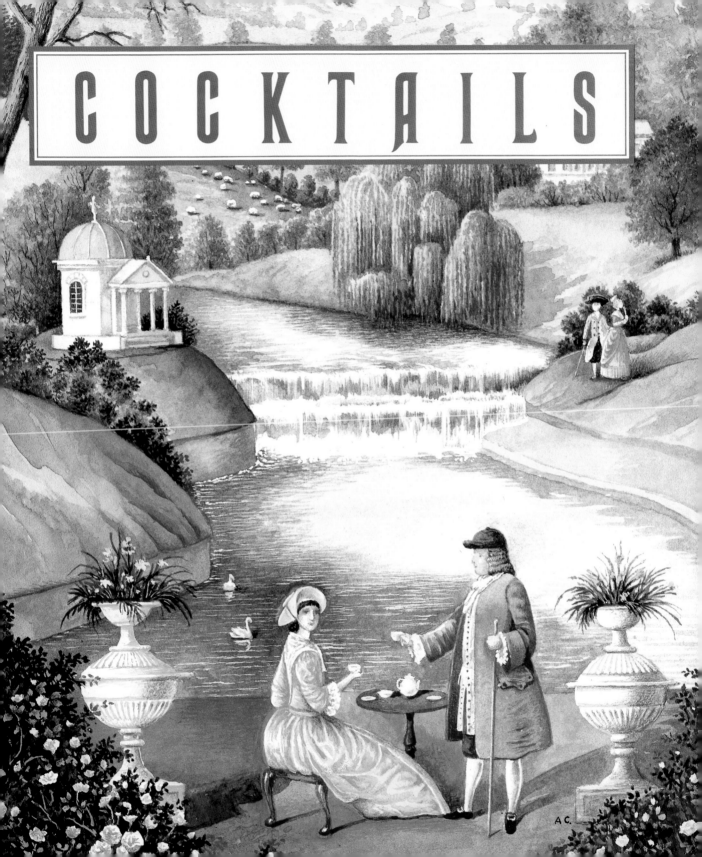

GARDEN PARTY

MENU

◆

*R*OSE BLOSSOM PUNCH

◆

*C*HERRY TOMATOES
FILLED WITH BLUE
CHEESE

◆

*T*ORTELLINI WITH
CORIANDER PESTO

◆

*W*ILD MUSHROOM
PROFITEROLES

◆

*C*RAB PHYLLO PURSES

◆

*B*ACON POLENTA
SQUARES

◆

*H*UMMUS WITH OLIVES

◆

*F*RUIT KEBABS WITH
MINT AND
HORSERADISH DIPPING
SAUCE

OPPOSITE: ROSE BLOSSOM PUNCH

ROSE BLOSSOM PUNCH

THIS LIGHT, FRESH-TASTING DRINK LOOKS STUNNING SERVED FROM A glass punch bowl. A rose-filled block of ice floating in the punch keeps it chilled at serving time.

3 pink unsprayed roses, with about 15 cm/6 inch stems, rinsed
2 litres/3½ pints dry white wine, chilled
125 ml/4 fl oz Kirsch

1 to 2 tablespoons rosewater
TO SERVE
Small pink unsprayed rose petals and leaves, rinsed and patted dry

The day before you plan to serve the punch, prepare the rose-filled ice cube for the centre of the punch bowl. To do so, thoroughly rinse out a 2 litre/3½ pint cardboard carton with water. Cut off top and trim top of sides to about 17.5 cm/7 inches. Place roses in carton. Fill to within 2.5 cm/1 inch of top with boiled and cooled water. Freeze overnight, or until solidly frozen.

To make the punch, combine wine, Kirsch and rosewater in a wide glass punch bowl. Remove cardboard from the rose-studded ice cube and place cube in the centre of punch bowl. Float small rose petals and leaves on top of punch. Serve punch in clear, long-stemmed wine glasses.

— 16 SERVINGS —

CHERRY TOMATOES FILLED WITH BLUE CHEESE

THE MILDNESS OF DANISH BLUE CHEESE MARRIES WELL WITH TART tomatoes, whereas the stronger flavour of Stilton is delicious with sweeter varieties of tomato.

25 small cherry tomatoes, stalks removed
FILLING
125 g/4 oz Danish blue cheese or Stilton
125 g/4 oz cream cheese

2 tablespoons double cream
2 tablespoons grated onion
TO ASSEMBLE
Salt
Freshly ground pepper
Snipped chives

Cut tomatoes in half horizontally and carefully scoop seeds out of each half with a demitasse spoon or small melon-ball cutter. Place scooped out halves upside-down on kitchen paper to drain.

Combine blue cheese, cream cheese, cream and onion in a mixing bowl or food processor and beat with an electric mixer or process until thoroughly blended.

Invert tomato halves and season cavities with salt and pepper. Spoon cheese mixture into a piping bag fitted with a star tube and pipe it into each tomato half. Garnish with chives and arrange on a platter.

— MAKES 50 HORS D'OEUVRES —

$\mathcal{T}$ORTELLINI WITH CORIANDER PESTO

THE SAUCE, WHICH CAN BE MADE IN ADVANCE, OWES ITS INSPIRATION to *pesto*, the classic Ligurian mixture of basil, pine nuts, olive oil and Pecorino cheese.

CORIANDER PESTO
30	g/1 oz dry roasted peanuts
1	shallot, quartered
60	g/2 oz flat-leaf parsley leaves
45	g/1½ oz fresh coriander leaves
175	ml/6 fl oz light olive oil
2	tablespoons red wine vinegar
	Salt
	Freshly ground pepper

PASTA
250 g/8 oz fresh cheese-filled tortellini
250 g/8 oz fresh spinach-filled tortellini

Bring a large pan of salted water to the boil.

Meanwhile, in a food processor pulse peanuts, shallot, parsley and coriander with an on/off motion to produce a coarse paste. With the motor on, drizzle oil and vinegar through the feed tube. Add salt and pepper to taste and process briefly to blend.

Add tortellini to boiling water, let water return to the boil and cook for 5 to 8 minutes, or until pasta is tender but still slightly firm, or *al dente*.

Drain pasta in a colander and return it to pan. Add sauce and toss gently to coat pasta well.

To serve, turn pasta into a shallow serving bowl or platter. Serve with a small glass of cocktail sticks for spearing and eating the pasta.

— 8 COCKTAIL SERVINGS —

This green sauce also flavours chicken wonderfully. Slip the fingers under the skin on the breast of a roasting chicken to form a large pocket on either side of the breastbone. Spoon the sauce into the pockets and rub the outside of the skin to spread the mixture evenly.

Roast the chicken in the usual way. Every slice of white meat will have a sliver of the aromatic seasoning, and if there is a spoonful or so left over, stir this into the gravy. Half-quantities are adequate for a 2.7 kg/6 lb chicken.

WILD MUSHROOM PROFITEROLES

THE PROFITEROLES SHOULD BE FILLED JUST BEFORE SERVING, BUT both the pastries and the filling can be made early in the day and reheated. Reheat the profiteroles in a 150° C/300° F/Gas 2 oven for a few minutes until re-crisped. Heat the filling gently in a bowl set over hot water before spooning or piping into profiteroles.

CHOUX PASTRY

60 g/ 2 oz unsalted butter
Salt
Freshly ground white pepper
140 g/5 oz plain flour
4 size 3 eggs

MUSHROOM FILLING

30 g/1 oz dried wild mushrooms such as ceps, funghi, porcini or morels (see Note)
250 g/8 oz cultivated, white mushrooms
3 tablespoons unsalted butter
2 large shallots, finely chopped
2 tablespoons chopped fresh tarragon, or 2 teaspoons dried
125 ml/4 fl oz double cream
Pinch freshly grated nutmeg
1 to 2 teaspoons fresh lemon juice
1 tablespoon chopped flat-leaf parsley
Salt
Freshly ground pepper

TO FINISH

40 whole flat-leaf parsley leaves

Prepare the *choux* pastry: Preheat oven to 200° C/400° F/Gas 6. In a heavy saucepan, combine butter with 125 ml/4 fl oz water and season with a pinch each of salt and white pepper. Bring to a rolling boil, reduce heat to low and add flour all at once, stirring vigorously until mixture pulls away from the side of the pan and forms a ball. Remove from the heat and let cool slightly. Add 3 of the eggs, one at a time, beating vigorously for 1 to 2 minutes after each addition until batter becomes smooth and satiny. In a small bowl beat remaining egg with 1 teaspoon water to form an egg wash and set aside.

Drop the batter by teaspoonful about 5 cm/2 inches apart on to lightly buttered baking sheets to form small mounds or spoon batter into a piping bag fitted with a plain 9 mm/⅜ inch tube and pipe mounds on to baking sheets. (Mounds should be about 2 cm/¾ inch in diameter.) Brush the tops of the mounds lightly with the egg wash. Bake in the centre of the oven for 15 to 20 minutes, or until buns are puffed, golden brown and hollow in the middle. Let cool on wire racks.

While the pastry is baking, brush away any dirt that clings to the wild mushrooms and place the mushrooms in a small bowl. Add enough boiling water to cover and set aside to soak for 30 minutes. Turn the wild mushrooms into a sieve lined with a double layer of muslin set over a small saucepan to catch the soaking liquid. Thoroughly rinse mushrooms, removing any remaining dirt or debris, and place in the bowl of a food processor. Place the saucepan with mushrooms' soaking liquid over medium heat and simmer until reduced to about 2 tablespoons.

Add cultivated mushrooms to the wild mushrooms in the food processor and pulse with on/off motion until all are finely chopped.

In a large frying pan, melt the butter over medium-low heat, add shallots and cook for 1 minute. Add mushrooms, their reduced liquid and the tarragon. Cook over medium heat, stirring frequently, until all liquid has evaporated, approximately 5 minutes. Stir in cream and nutmeg and simmer over low heat, stirring frequently, for about 15 minutes, or until the cream is entirely absorbed by the mushrooms. Season with lemon juice, chopped parsley, salt and pepper and keep mixture warm.

To assemble, make a small slit on the side of each profiterole and spoon about 1 teaspoon of the filling into the centre. (A piping bag may also be used.) Arrange a parsley leaf on the filling of each profiterole so that it extends over the edge, pat the tops in place, and arrange the profiteroles on a platter.

— MAKES ABOUT 40 PROFITEROLES —

Note: If fresh wild mushrooms are available, substitute 150 g/5 oz of them for the 30 g/1 oz dried mushrooms.

This filling is delicious and versatile. For a change, spread it thickly on fingers of white toast. Grill the toast fingers for 2 to 3 minutes, or until the mushroom mixture is heated through, and serve them as hors d'oeuvres. The filling can also be used in savoury crêpes, or it can be spooned into large mushroom caps that have first been lightly sautéed. Grill the stuffed mushrooms for about 5 minutes, so that the filling is hot but the caps are not overcooked.

CRAB PHYLLO PURSES

Phyllo sheets are a great ally to the cook, whether assembled in the traditional streudel form or in bite-size purses. Fillings

PHYLLO PASTRY IS EASY TO HANDLE AS LONG AS THE STACK OF UNUSED sheets is kept covered with a damp tea towel to prevent drying while the purses are being assembled. The purses may be prepared to the point of baking, then frozen in a single layer on the baking sheet. If baking them from the frozen state, add about 5 minutes to the cooking time.

175 g/6 oz unsalted butter
6   tablespoons finely chopped spring onion
2   tablespoons dry vermouth
4   teaspoons Dijon mustard
4   tablespoons finely chopped parsley
2   tablespoons finely chopped fresh dill, or
      2 teaspoons dried
4   drops Tabasco or other hot pepper sauce
¼   teaspoon Worcestershire sauce
250 g/8 oz fresh white crab meat
4   tablespoons *crème fraîche* or soured cream
      Salt
      Freshly ground pepper
6   sheets phyllo pastry dough (30 × 40 cm/12 × 16 inches each)
4   tablespoons dry breadcrumbs
1   tablespoon freshly grated Parmesan cheese

should be reasonably firm and can include fish, meat or vegetable mixtures as well as fruit combinations for pies.

The wild mushroom filling for profiteroles on page 158 is a fine purse-filler, if a further 75 g/ 2½ oz coarsely chopped mushrooms are added to the finely chopped ones.

Melt 125 g/4 oz of the butter in a small saucepan over very low heat and set aside.

Melt remaining butter in a medium frying pan, add spring onions and cook over medium-low heat until softened, about 3 minutes. Stir in vermouth and mustard and cook, stirring, about 2 minutes. Add parsley, dill, Tabasco, Worcestershire sauce, crab meat and *crème fraîche*. Season with salt and pepper and stir to blend thoroughly. Remove from the heat and let cool to room temperature.

Preheat oven to 190° C/375° F/Gas 5.

Spread phyllo sheets out on a flat surface between 2 slightly damp tea towels. In a small bowl, combine breadcrumbs and cheese.

Carefully remove one sheet of phyllo and place on another damp towel on a flat surface (re-covering remaining phyllo), brush it with melted butter, then sprinkle lightly with some of the breadcrumb mixture. Fold phyllo in half to form a 20 × 30 cm/8 × 12 inch rectangle. Brush again with butter. Using a sharp knife, cut phyllo into six

10 cm/4 inch squares. Mound about 1½ teaspoons crab meat filling in the centre of each square. Then carefully gather up edges of squares with your fingers and pinch together in the centres to form plump 'purses.' Brush the centres and edges with butter to prevent drying and cracking and place purses on a lightly buttered baking sheet. Repeat the procedure with remaining 5 phyllo sheets, bread crumb mixture and filling, to make 36 purses.

Bake in centre of oven for 12 to 15 minutes, or until lightly golden and crisp. Transfer to wire racks to cool slightly.

Serve warm or at room temperature.

— MAKES 36 HORS D'OEUVRES —

Fruit Kebabs with Mint and Horseradish Dipping Sauce

THIS RECIPE REQUIRES THE BEST OF THE SUMMER'S RIPE FRUITS. THE greater the variety of fruit used, the more colourful and attractive this presentation will be.

100 to 120 cubes of fresh summer fruits such as rock or
    Charentais melon, watermelon, honeydew melon,
    peaches, kiwi, and strawberries
175 ml/6 fl oz double cream
3 tablespoons chopped fresh mint leaves
2 teaspoons freshly grated horseradish or well-
    drained bottled horseradish

TO SERVE
2 large bunches fresh mint
30 wooden skewers (15 cm/6 inches long)

Thread 3 or 4 cubes of different types and colours of fruit on to each of the wooden skewers.

In a small bowl, beat cream just until soft peaks form and fold in chopped mint and horseradish. Pour dipping sauce into a serving bowl that is shallow and wide enough for skewers to be dipped lengthways.

Arrange a bed of mint sprigs on a basket or large tray and pile fruit skewers attractively on mint. Or stick skewers into a Charentais or watermelon half in the centre of a round platter decorated with mint sprigs. Serve fruit skewers with sauce.

— MAKES 30 HORS D'OEUVRES —

Fruit cubes on skewers with a bowl of whipped cream sugared to taste and sharpened with rum make a light, simple dessert for informal meals throughout the year.

BACON POLENTA SQUARES

The chilled polenta can
also be cut into 5 cm/
2 inch rounds arranged
in overlapping circles in a
fairly shallow round
baking dish, sprinkled
with grated cheese and
baked as for the squares.
Serve with a mushroom
or tomato sauce, accom-
panied by a green salad
and French bread.

250 g/8 oz streaky bacon rashers
1   to 2 tablespoons vegetable oil
175 g/6 oz cornmeal
1   teaspoon salt
¾   teaspoon freshly ground pepper
    Pinch grated nutmeg
300 g/10 oz mature Cheddar cheese, grated
4   teaspoons finely chopped fresh thyme leaves, or
    1½ teaspoons dried

TO SERVE
Fresh thyme sprigs

In a large frying pan, sauté bacon in oil over medium heat until crisp.
Drain on kitchen paper. Crumble bacon and set aside.

Fill a large heavy saucepan with 750 ml/1¼ pints water and bring to
the boil. Meanwhile, place cornmeal in a bowl with 600 ml/1 pint water
and stir to blend well. Stir moistened cornmeal into boiling water,
reduce heat to medium-low and cook, stirring almost constantly with a
wooden spoon, for 20 minutes, or until mixture is very thick and begins
to pull away from the side of the pan. Remove from heat and stir in salt,
pepper, nutmeg, bacon, 125 g/4 oz of the cheese and 2 teaspoons of the
thyme leaves.

While still warm, pour the polenta mixture into a well-buttered 25 ×
12.5 cm/10 × 5 inch Swiss roll tin or rimmed baking tray. Spread mixture out as evenly as possible with a rubber spatula and smooth the top.
(Mixture should be about 5 mm/¼ inch thick.) Set aside to cool to room
temperature. Then chill in the refrigerator until firm and set, at least 1
hour. (If not baking immediately, cover polenta with polythene when
chilled and set.)

Preheat oven to 200° C/400° F/Gas 6.

Sprinkle remaining cheese and thyme leaves over top of chilled
polenta. Bake in centre of oven for 25 to 30 minutes, or until cheese is
melted and bubbly and the polenta is beginning to brown around the
edges. Remove from oven and let cool in the tin for 10 minutes before
cutting. Cut into 5 equal strips lengthways and 10 across.

To serve, arrange in a napkin-lined basket or tray, garnish with thyme
sprigs and serve warm.

— MAKES 50 HORS D'OEUVRES —

Hummus with Olives

FRESHLY COOKED DRIED CHICK PEAS PRODUCE THE BEST FLAVOUR BUT must be soaked in water to cover by 7.5 cm/3 inches and chilled overnight before cooking. Good canned chick peas may be substituted. Crudités such as pepper strips and carrot and celery sticks may be substituted for the pitta bread.

175	g/6 oz dried chick peas, soaked (see Note)
5½	tablespoons sesame paste (tahini)
4	tablespoons fresh lemon juice
4	tablespoons olive oil
2	cloves garlic, finely chopped
1½	teaspoons salt
¼	teaspoon ground cumin
¼	teaspoon freshly ground pepper
15	g/½ oz flat-leaf parsley, chopped
60	g/2 oz stoned black olives, finely chopped

TO SERVE
6   pitta bread pockets or 48 plain savoury biscuits
Flat-leaf parsley sprigs

Drain chick peas in a colander. In a medium saucepan, combine peas with enough water to cover by 5 cm/2 inches and bring to the boil over medium-high heat. Reduce heat to low, cover saucepan and simmer for 1½ to 2 hours, or until chick peas are tender. Drain in the colander and let cool.

Combine chick peas, sesame paste, lemon juice, olive oil, garlic, salt, cumin and pepper in a food processor or blender and process until smooth and slightly fluffy, about 30 to 45 seconds. Add chopped parsley and olives and process with on/off motion just until well blended.

Preheat grill.

Split pitta bread into 2 rounds and cut into quarters, then place on a baking sheet and grill until lightly toasted. Meanwhile, scoop hummus into a serving bowl and garnish with parsley sprigs. Arrange toasted pitta bread on a platter around the hummus.

— MAKES 600 ML/1 PINT HUMMUS AND 48 HORS D'OEUVRES —

Note: If using canned chick peas, use a 540 g/19 oz can and drain well. Reduce salt to 1 teaspoon.

Sesame paste, or tahini, can also be mixed with enough water to give the consistency of double cream. Season it with mashed garlic, lemon juice and salt and serve this dressing in a bowl to be spooned over a Greek mixed salad of lettuce, tomatoes, black olives, pepper and feta cheese. This makes an ideal salad to accompany barbecued meat.

AN INFORMAL DRINKS PARTY

MENU

◆

*P*IMM'S

◆

*G*LAZED CHICKEN
WINGS

◆

*F*RAGRANT CRUSHED
OLIVES

◆

*C*APONATA PIZZAS

◆

*S*ESAME-CHEESE
WAFERS

◆

*M*USSELS WITH
AVOCADO SAUCE

◆

*M*INIATURE TOMATO
AND MOZZARELLA
KEBABS

◆

*N*ECTARINES WITH
CHÈVRE, GORGONZOLA
AND PISTACHIOS

OPPOSITE: PIMM'S, MUSSELS WITH
AVOCADO SAUCE, FRAGRANT CRUSHED
OLIVES, CAPONATA PIZZAS, SESAME-
CHEESE WAFERS

Pimm's

THIS AMBER MIXTURE WITH ITS FLAMBOYANT DECORATION IS ONE OF the most summery and pleasant English drinks. A different spirit is used in each variety of Pimm's. Pimm's No. 1 contains gin; others contain whisky, rum or brandy.

500 ml/16 fl oz Pimm's No. 1
1   to 1.5 litres/2 to 2½ pints chilled fizzy
      lemonade or ginger ale
      Ice cubes

TO SERVE
4   to 6 thin slices orange, halved
8   to 12 thin slices lemon
8   to 12 thin slices cucumber
8   to 12 sprigs fresh mint
8   to 12 sprigs fresh borage

In a large jug, combine Pimm's and carbonated drink. Add enough ice cubes to chill mixture well. At serving time, pour mixture into tall glasses or clear mugs. Garnish each drink with a half slice orange, a slice each of lemon and cucumber, and a sprig each of mint and borage.

— MAKES 8 TO 12 DRINKS —

Glazed chicken wings

PREPARE AND COOK THESE SPICY CHICKEN WINGS EARLY IN THE DAY and serve them at room temperature. Or grill them just before serving time to serve hot. Other chicken joints may also be marinated in the spicy sauce and barbecued or grilled.

2   kg/4 lb chicken wings
      BARBECUE SAUCE
125 ml/4 fl oz (165 g/5½ oz)
      molasses
3   tablespoons sherry vinegar
2   tablespoons vegetable oil

1   teaspoon Worcestershire sauce
1   teaspoon coarsely ground black
      pepper
1   tablespoon Dijon mustard
½   teaspoon Tabasco sauce
½   teaspoon salt

Cut off wing tips and halve chicken wings at joints. Arrange wing pieces in a single layer in a shallow baking dish.

In a heavy saucepan, combine molasses, vinegar, oil, Worcestershire sauce, pepper, mustard, Tabasco and salt. Simmer over medium heat for 6 to 8 minutes, stirring occasionally. Pour sauce over the chicken pieces, cover and refrigerate for about 3 hours, turning chicken 2 or 3 times.

About 30 minutes before cooking time, remove chicken from refrigerator and set aside to come to room temperature.

Build a medium-hot charcoal fire or preheat grill. Arrange chicken pieces on a barbecue grid or grill pan about 10 cm/4 inches from heat and cook for 6 to 8 minutes on each side, brushing several times with remaining sauce until chicken is crisp, browned and cooked through but still moist.

Arrange on a serving platter.

— MAKES 48 HORS D'OEUVRES —

For a spicier, less sweet glaze, marinate and baste the chicken wings with 175 to 250 ml/6 to 8 fl oz Crabtree & Evelyn Cabshelter Sauce.

This rich, spicy sauce was originated in the "shelters" that traditionally served meat pies, potatoes and brown sauce to Victorian cabbies.

ℱRAGRANT CRUSHED OLIVES

THESE SEASONED OLIVES WILL BE MOST DELICIOUS IF THEY ARE PRE-pared a day in advance to allow the flavour to develop. To keep them for several days or longer, place olives and seasonings in a jar, add enough light vegetable oil to cover (olive oil is not necessary) and store in a cool place.

```
500 g/1 lb   small unstoned green olives
1            tablespoon coriander seeds
1            clove garlic, thinly sliced
4            to 5 thin slices lemon, each cut into 6 wedges
```

In a mixing bowl, combine olives, coriander seeds, garlic and lemon wedges and stir to blend. Transfer mixture to a heavy polythene bag and seal tightly. Place bag on a work surface so that olives are in a single layer and, using a rolling pin or wooden mallet, gently hit olives to crush them slightly without breaking bag. Place bag in the refrigerator overnight.

Transfer olives and their seasonings to an attractive dish and serve.

— MAKES 500 G/1 LB —

After the flavours have matured, these olives can be stoned, sliced and added to stuffings for fish or chicken or to mixed green salads.

CAPONATA PIZZAS

THE AUBERGINE NEED NOT BE PEELED, AS THE SKIN LENDS ITS RICH colour to the *caponata*. The vegetable mixture may be made up to 3 days in advance or the entire pizzas made ahead and frozen. Reheat the pizzas for about 20 minutes in a 150° C/300° F/Gas 2 oven before serving.

Caponata can also be served at room temperature on savoury biscuits, hot as an accompaniment to simple egg dishes or as a filling for an omelet, and hot or cold as a light relish with fish and meats.

To make a quicker base, make up the Currant Cream Scones on page 140, omitting the currants and sugar. When baked, split them open horizontally, spread each half with the caponata, *and grill them for 2 to 3 minutes, or until the ca-ponata is heated through.*

CAPONATA
3 tablespoons olive oil
250 g/8 oz aubergine (preferably very small), cut into 1 cm/½ inch cubes
1 medium onion, thinly sliced
1 stick of celery, thinly sliced
1 small red pepper, cored, seeded, and thinly sliced
1 clove garlic, finely chopped
250 g/8 oz ripe tomatoes, peeled, seeded and diced
30 g/1 oz stoned Greek olives, sliced
1 tablespoon red wine vinegar
   Pinch caster sugar
1 bay leaf
1 teaspoon chopped fresh thyme, or ¼ teaspoon dried
1 tablespoon chopped fresh basil
   Salt
   Freshly ground black pepper
2 tablespoons chopped fresh parsley
1 tablespoon drained capers

PIZZA DOUGH
385 g/13½ oz strong bread flour
7 g/¼ oz easy-blend dried yeast
¼ teaspoon caster sugar
1 teaspoon salt
4 tablespoons olive oil
   Cornmeal (for baking sheet)

In a large frying pan, combine oil, aubergine, onion, celery and red pepper and sauté over medium heat for about 4 minutes, or until softened. Add garlic and cook, stirring for about 1 minute. Stir in tomatoes, olives, vinegar, sugar, bay leaf, thyme and basil and season with salt and pepper. Cover and simmer over low heat, stirring often, for about 20 minutes, or until vegetables are very soft. Remove cover and

continue to simmer over low heat, stirring frequently, for 15 to 20 minutes, or until most of the liquid has evaporated. Stir in parsley and capers. Taste and correct seasoning if necessary. Remove *caponata* from heat and let cool.

Meanwhile, prepare pizza dough: In a large bowl, stir together 245 g/8¾ oz of the flour, the yeast, sugar and salt. In a saucepan, heat 1 tablespoon of the olive oil with 250 ml/8 fl oz water until hot to the touch (40° to 45° C/105° to 115° F). Stir the liquid into the dry ingredients, then incorporate enough of the remaining flour to make a soft but workable dough. Knead for about 10 minutes, until the dough is smooth and elastic. Place in an oiled bowl, turning dough to coat it, cover with a damp cloth and let rise in a warm place until double in bulk, about 30 minutes. Knock back dough and divide into 24 equal pieces.

Preheat oven to 250° C/500° F/Gas 9 to 10.

On a lightly floured work surface, roll out each piece of dough into a thin round, about 7.5 cm/3 inches in diameter. Sprinkle a baking sheet lightly with cornmeal and arrange 6 to 8 rounds of dough on it. Use remaining 3 tablespoons olive oil to brush the dough rounds lightly. Spread about 1 tablespoon of *caponata* evenly over each pizza, leaving a 1 cm/½ inch border around the edge. Let pizzas stand for about 5 minutes before baking.

Bake in lower third of oven for 8 to 10 minutes, or until bottoms of pizzas are browned and crisp and tops are puffed and golden. Meanwhile, prepare the next baking sheet of pizzas for the oven. Continue in this manner until all are baked.

Serve warm or at room temperature.

— MAKES 24 INDIVIDUAL PIZZAS —

Sesame-Cheese Wafers

Cheddar and Stilton combine beautifully. The proof: mash some Stilton with an equal amount of softened unsalted butter and spread the mixture on these Cheddar wafers.

THIS SIMPLE AND VERY GOOD ACCOMPANIMENT TO DRINKS CAN BE made even more easily by omitting the second dipping of the wafers in the sesame seeds, in which case only 2 tablespoons sesame seeds are needed. The uncooked roll of dough can be frozen and thawed shortly before baking.

4	tablespoons sesame seeds
140	g/5 oz plain flour
½	teaspoon baking powder
¼	teaspoon salt
60	g/2 oz cold unsalted butter, cut into small pieces
90	g/3 oz mature Cheddar cheese, grated

Preheat oven to 180° C/350° F/Gas 4. Spread the sesame seeds over a baking sheet and toast for about 10 minutes, or until they are lightly coloured and fragrant. Remove from the oven and set aside to cool.

Combine flour, baking powder and salt in a food processor and pulse to blend. Add butter and cheese and process until mixture resembles coarse crumbs. Add 2 tablespoons cold water and process until mixture forms a ball, adding ½ tablespoon more water if necessary to make dough hold together.

Shape dough into a log about 4 cm/1½ inches in diameter. Spread the toasted sesame seeds on a sheet of greaseproof paper and roll the log in the sesame seeds until the surface is covered. Wrap log in cling film and chill for at least 2 hours or overnight. Place remaining sesame seeds in a small dish.

Preheat the oven to 220° C/425° F/Gas 7.

With a sharp knife, cut dough log into 3 mm/⅛ inch thick slices. Dip one side of each wafer in the remaining sesame seeds to cover and place wafers, seeded-sides-up and spaced slightly apart, on ungreased baking sheets. Bake wafers for 7 to 10 minutes, or until nicely golden and let cool on wire racks.

— MAKES ABOUT 48 WAFERS —

Mussels with Avocado Sauce

THE AVOCADO SAUCE IS ALSO SUPERB ON SLICED TOMATOES OR OVER A platter of fresh prawns.

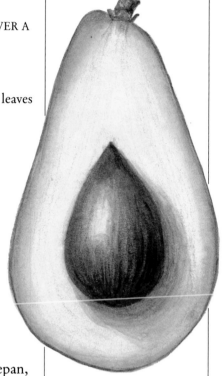

1.5 g/3 lb mussels (about 48)
125 ml/4 fl oz dry white wine
1 teaspoon finely chopped shallot
1 bay leaf

SAUCE
1 medium ripe avocado
1 tablespoon fresh lemon juice
1 small fresh green chilli, cored, seeded and chopped
½ small green pepper, cored, seeded and chopped
4 tablespoons sliced spring onion (white with some green)
1 tablespoon chopped fresh coriander leaves
1 clove garlic, finely chopped
⅛ teaspoon ground cumin
  Salt
  Freshly ground black pepper

TO SERVE
48 small fresh coriander leaves
  Lemon wedges

Thoroughly scrub mussel shells and remove beards. In a large saucepan, combine mussels with the wine, shallot, bay leaf and 125 ml/4 fl oz water. Cover, bring liquid to the boil and steam mussels over medium-low heat for 4 to 5 minutes, or until mussels open. Remove from heat and let cool slightly, discarding any mussels that did not open. Remove mussels from their shells, tearing off and discarding half of each shell and placing other half in a colander. Rinse shells thoroughly to remove grit, pat them dry and return mussels to cleaned half shells. Arrange in a spiral or concentric circles pattern on a large round serving platter.

In a small bowl, mash avocado with lemon juice, then beat to a smooth purée. Stir in the chilli, pepper, spring onion, chopped coriander, garlic and cumin, season with salt and pepper and stir until well blended.

Spoon about 1 teaspoon avocado sauce over each mussel. Garnish with a coriander leaf, place lemon wedges in centre of the platter and serve.

— MAKES ABOUT 48 HORS D'OEUVRES —

MINIATURE TOMATO AND MOZZARELLA KEBABS

The main ingredients here can be the makings of a summery salad in the colours of the Italian flag. Slice the mozzarella 5 mm/¼ inch thick and the tomatoes 1 cm/ ½ inch thick. Arrange them with basil sprigs, alternating and overlapping them, on a serving dish and dress the salad simply with a mixture of 1 tablespoon sherry vinegar, 3 to 5 tablespoons olive oil, and salt and pepper to taste.

THE SKEWERS OF CHEESE AND TOMATO MAY BE ASSEMBLED SEVERAL hours ahead, wrapped tightly and refrigerated. Bring to room temperature before dressing and serving.

250 g/8 oz	mozzarella cheese, cut into 1 cm/½ inch cubes
3	to 4 unpeeled ripe tomatoes, seeded and cut into 2 cm/¾ inch cubes
1	large bunch fresh basil (see Note)
3	tablespoons olive oil
2	teaspoons red wine vinegar
½	teaspoon Dijon mustard
	Salt
	Freshly ground pepper

Thread 1 cube of cheese and 1 cube of tomato on to each of 45 wooden cocktail sticks.

Shred enough of the fresh basil leaves to make about 2 tablespoons and set aside. Use the remaining basil leaves to line a serving platter. Arrange cheese and tomato skewers on the bed of basil.

In a small bowl, whisk together oil, vinegar and mustard until emulsified.

Just before serving, drizzle vinaigrette evenly over skewers, sprinkle shredded basil over cheese and tomato skewers and season lightly with salt and freshly ground pepper.

— MAKES 45 HORS D'OEUVRES —

Note: If fresh basil is not available, replace the 2 tablespoons fresh with 2 teaspoons dried and line the platter with fresh parsley.

Nectarines with Chèvre, Gorgonzola and Pistachios

THIS IS A DO-IT-YOURSELF HORS D'OEUVRE FOR AN INFORMAL SUMMER drinks party. If the blended cheeses seem a bit too thick to spread easily, thin them with a teaspoon or so of cream or milk.

90	g/3 oz goat's cheese (chèvre), softened
45	g/1½ oz Gorgonzola cheese, softened
4	ripe nectarines
	Fresh lemon juice
45	g/1½ oz shelled pistachios, chopped

Combine goat's cheese and Gorgonzola in a small bowl and beat until thoroughly blended and smooth.

Cut 1 nectarine in half, remove stone, and cut each half into 2 or 3 bite-size wedges. Brush cut sides of fruit lightly with lemon juice. Spread a little of the cheese mixture in the indentation of each nectarine wedge. Then top each wedge with chopped pistachios to coat cheese lightly.

Transfer remaining cheese mixture to a small glass serving bowl. Place remaining pistachios in a small shallow serving bowl. Arrange the prepared fruit wedges, the 3 remaining uncut nectarines and the bowls of cheese and pistachios on a large serving platter or wooden board, along with small knives for cutting the fruit and spreading the cheese. The prepared fruit wedges will serve as examples, showing guests how to slice, spread and top the remaining nectarines themselves. (Remaining nectarines need not be brushed with lemon juice.)

— MAKES 16 TO 24 HORS D'OEUVRES —

PUTTING ON THE RITZ

MENU

◆

*K*IR ROYALE

◆

*P*RAWN CANAPÉS WITH
FENNEL BUTTER

◆

*C*HICKEN LIVER AND
OLIVE PÂTÉ

◆

*C*ELERY BOATS WITH
CHÈVRE AND WALNUTS

◆

*V*EGETABLES WITH
SAFFRON-CHILLI
MAYONNAISE

◆

*G*RILLED LAMB CUBES
WITH PAPAYA

◆

*Q*UAIL'S EGGS WRAPPED
IN ROASTED PEPPERS

◆

*B*LINIS WITH HERBS,
SALMON ROE AND
SOURED CREAM

◆

*W*HITE HAZELNUT
FRUITCAKE

OPPOSITE: BLINIS WITH HERBS, SALMON
ROE AND SOURED CREAM, PRAWN
CANAPÉS WITH FENNEL BUTTER AND
KIR ROYALE

$\mathcal{K}$IR ROYALE

SPARKLING AND FESTIVE, THIS IS A VARIATION ON THE CLASSIC KIR made with white Burgundy and crème de cassis. Measure the blackcurrant liqueur into glasses in advance and pour the Champagne in at the last moment: it will blend with the cassis with no stirring necessary.

125 ml/4 fl oz crème de cassis
2   bottles Champagne, chilled
12 to 14 thin curls of lemon zest (optional)

Pour 2 teaspoons cassis into each Champagne flute. Fill glasses three-quarters full with Champagne. Drop a curl of lemon zest into each glass.

— MAKES 12 TO 14 DRINKS —

$\mathcal{P}$RAWN CANAPÉS WITH FENNEL BUTTER

THE CANAPÉS MAY BE ASSEMBLED 2 TO 3 HOURS AHEAD, BUT THE fennel sprigs should be added just before serving. Prepare the fennel butter at least 1 day ahead—or as many as 3 days—so that the flavours develop. Its light texture and delicate taste make it an excellent seasoning for vegetables and fish. To have a supply on hand, shape the butter into a log, wrap and refrigerate it until set, slice into 5 mm/¼ inch thick pats (keeping the log shape), then rewrap well and freeze. Thaw and use the individual pats as needed.

350 g/12 oz raw medium prawns (about 50) in their
    shells

FENNEL MARINADE
125 ml/4 fl oz light olive oil
2   tablespoons white wine vinegar
1   tablespoon fresh lemon juice
2   teaspoons Pernod or other anise-flavoured liqueur
2   teaspoons Dijon mustard
1   clove garlic, halved
¾ teaspoon salt
¼ teaspoon crushed fennel seed
⅛ teaspoon freshly ground pepper

FENNEL BUTTER

20 g/⅔ oz fennel leaves
10 g/⅓ oz fresh parsley leaves
250 g/8 oz unsalted butter, softened
1 tablespoon fresh lemon juice
1 tablespoon Pernod or other anise-flavoured liqueur
¾ teaspoon salt
⅛ teaspoon cayenne pepper
175 g/6 oz bulb fennel, finely chopped

TO ASSEMBLE

25 thin slices firm white sandwich bread
Fennel sprigs

Bring a large saucepan of lightly salted water to the boil, add prawns and boil for about 2 minutes, or until they turn pink. Turn prawns into a colander, refresh under cold water to stop cooking and drain. Remove shells and use a small knife to remove black veins from prawns. Carefully slice each prawn in half lengthways and set aside in a shallow glass or other non-reactive dish.

In a small bowl, stir together oil, vinegar, lemon juice, Pernod, mustard, garlic, salt, fennel seed and pepper until well blended. Pour marinade over prawns and chill in the refrigerator for at least 2 hours or up to 8 hours, turning once or twice.

To prepare fennel butter, finely chop fennel and parsley leaves in a food processor, add butter and process until well combined. With the motor running, add lemon juice and Pernod through the feed tube. Season with salt and cayenne and stir in the bulb fennel.

To assemble, remove prawns from the marinade and pat dry on kitchen paper. Spread each bread slice with fennel butter (butter should be room temperature). Using a 4 cm/1½ inch round biscuit cutter, cut 4 rounds from each bread slice or cut bread into 4 squares. Place a prawn half, pink side up, on each canapé, cover loosely with polythene, and chill in the refrigerator for at least 20 minutes to firm butter. To serve, garnish each canapé with a fennel sprig and arrange on a serving platter.

— MAKES 100 HORS D'OEUVRES —

The French canon, Félix Kir, eminent cleric, mayor of Dijon and distinguished member of the French Resistance during World War II, may be longest remembered for inventing the cooling apéritif that bears his name.

CHICKEN LIVER AND OLIVE PÂTÉ

THIS PÂTÉ CAN ALSO BE SERVED AS A FIRST COURSE AT DINNER ON buttered toast, in which case it looks particularly appetizing brought to the table in a pâté dish and covered with a thin layer of clarified butter (see sidebar) and a sprinkling of thyme.

350	g/12 oz chicken livers
2	tablespoons Madeira or medium sherry
2	tablespoons milk
125	g/4 oz unsalted butter
90	g/3 oz onion, chopped
2	tablespoons Cognac or other brandy
½	teaspoon salt
⅛	teaspoon freshly ground pepper
⅛	teaspoon ground mace
45	g/1½ oz stoned black olives, preferably Kalamata or Niçoise, slivered
1	box (200 g/7 oz) Crabtree & Evelyn Cream Crackers or other cream crackers

To make clarified butter, in a small saucepan melt 250 g/8 oz butter over low heat, remove it from the heat and let it stand for several minutes, or until the milky residue sinks to the bottom. Then pour the clear yellow butter into another container, taking care that none of the residue mixes with it. This butter keeps for weeks in the refrigerator and is also an excellent frying and sautéeing medium, as it burns less easily than unclarified butter.

Trim tough membranes and any yellow patches from chicken livers and separate each into 2 lobes. Let soak in a small bowl with Madeira and milk for at least 3 hours or overnight.

In a large frying pan, melt 15 g/½ oz of the butter, add onion and cook, stirring occasionally, over medium heat for 5 minutes, or until softened and lightly browned. Spoon onion into a food processor and set pan aside.

Pour off and discard soaking liquid from chicken livers and pat the livers dry on kitchen paper. Melt 30 g/1 oz of the remaining butter in pan in which onion was browned. When butter is hot, add chicken livers and sauté, stirring occasionally, over medium-high heat for about 5 minutes, or until browned and firm but still pale pink inside. Using a slotted spoon, transfer chicken livers to the food processor.

Remove pan from heat and add Cognac. Return pan to the stove, increase heat to high and cook, stirring to scrape up brown bits, for 3 minutes. Add pan juices to food processor.

Cut remaining butter into several pieces. Start processing chicken liver mixture, adding butter one piece at a time through feed tube until mixture is a smooth purée. Add salt, pepper and mace and continue to process until thoroughly blended and smooth. Transfer mixture to a bowl and stir in slivered olives. Taste and correct seasoning, if necessary. Pack the pâté into a crock, cover tightly and place in the refrigerator to chill for at least 4 hours or up to 2 to 3 days to allow flavours to develop and blend.

Remove pâté from refrigerator 1 hour before serving. Serve with cream crackers.

— MAKES ABOUT 30 HORS D'OEUVRES —

CELERY BOATS WITH CHÈVRE AND WALNUTS

CELERY, CHEESE AND BUTTER, ACCOMPANIED BY SAVOURY BISCUITS and a bowl of nuts, is a traditional ending to many lunches and dinners. This hors d'oeuvre includes the best flavours and textures of that combination. It can be prepared several hours in advance, covered with polythene, and refrigerated until half an hour before serving.

6   to 8 large celery sticks
250 g/8 oz goat's cheese (chèvre), softened
125 g/4 oz unsalted butter, softened
40   walnut halves
     TO SERVE
     Celery or fresh parsley leaves

Trim celery sticks, remove strings, rinse and pat dry. Trim off a thin lengthways strip along the rounded back of each stick to form a flat bottom.

Trim off and discard rind from the chèvre, if necessary, and blend cheese with butter in a food processor with an on/off motion until smooth.

Spoon cheese mixture into the hollows of celery, mounding it nicely, and top with walnut halves, spaced 1 cm/½ inch apart along the length of the celery. Using a sharp knife, cut on a sharp diagonal between walnuts to form bite-size pieces. Arrange on a serving platter and top each piece with a celery or parsley leaf.

— MAKES ABOUT 40 HORS D'OEUVRES —

VEGETABLES WITH SAFFRON-CHILLI MAYONNAISE

A lemony bagna cauda—or garlic and anchovy 'hot bath'—is a tempting optional sauce for these vegetables. In a small heavy saucepan, gently heat 125 ml/4 fl oz olive oil with 30 g/1 oz un-salted butter. Stir in 2 tablespoons lemon juice, 5 mashed anchovy fillets and 3 crushed garlic cloves. Simmer gently for 5 minutes. Pour the sauce (minus the garlic cloves) into a small pot or heatproof bowl set over a candle warmer. Put pot and warmer in the centre of a heatproof tray or wooden board and arrange the vegetables around it. Guests choose a vegeta-ble 'dipper' and swirl it in the sauce to keep the mixture well blended as it coats the vegetables.

CHOOSE A SELECTION OF BABY VEGETABLES AND/OR OTHERS THAT can be served whole or cut into bite-size pieces. The blanched vegetables are equally delicious warm or cold, arranged in Chinese steamer baskets or on any shallow basket or platter.

SAFFRON-CHILLI MAYONNAISE

3	tablespoons white wine vinegar
12	saffron threads (approximately)
2	size 3 egg yolks
1	small fresh hot red chilli, cored and seeded, or ¼ to ½ teaspoon cayenne pepper (see Note)
1	small clove garlic
¾	teaspoon salt
350	ml/12 fl oz olive oil
	Pinch sugar

750	g/1½ lb fresh baby vegetables or small, individual vegetables suitable for dipping such as beetroots, carrots, courgettes, mange-touts, sugar snap peas, green beans, asparagus spears, broccoli, cauliflower and new potatoes
	Salt
	Freshly ground black pepper
	Paprika

In a small saucepan, warm vinegar and 1 tablespoon water briefly over low heat, add crumbled saffron threads and remove pan from heat. Let saffron steep for 10 minutes.

In a food processor or a mixing bowl, process or briefly whisk egg yolks, saffron mixture, chilli, garlic and salt just until blended. Through feed tube or whisking vigorously by hand, add oil, a tablespoon at a time, until the mixture begins to thicken. Add remaining oil in a thin, steady stream, processing or whisking continuously until oil is thoroughly incorporated and mixture is quite thick and smooth. Add sugar, taste and add more salt if necessary, then blend again briefly to mix.

To prepare vegetables, rinse and drain, leaving on some of stalks of carrots and beetroots. Remove strings from mange-touts, sugar snap peas and green beans. Trim asparagus spears. Trim broccoli and cauli-flower into florets.

Bring to the boil a large pan of lightly salted water. Blanch vegetables separately or in logical groupings (mange-touts, sugar snaps, green beans and asparagus together; carrots and courgettes together; broccoli and cauliflower together, etc.) until just crisp-tender. Cooking times will vary: peas, beans and asparagus will need only 30 seconds; most others will require 1 to 2 minutes; new potatoes should cook for 5 to 8 minutes. Plunge vegetables as they are blanched into cold water to stop cooking and to set colour, then drain and pat dry thoroughly with kitchen paper. If not serving immediately, wrap vegetables in cling film and refrigerate.

To serve, arrange vegetables in Chinese steamer baskets or any other basket or serving platter and sprinkle lightly with salt and pepper. Transfer saffron-chilli mayonnaise to a small serving bowl, sprinkle lightly with paprika and serve with the blanched vegetables for dipping. If desired, vegetables can be steam-warmed over gently boiling water in a wok before serving.

— MAKES 30 TO 40 HORS D'OEUVRES (400 ML/14 FL OZ MAYONNAISE) —

Note: If chilli or cayenne pepper is unavailable, replace 60 to 125 ml/2 to 4 fl oz of the olive oil in the recipe with an equal amount of Crabtree & Evelyn's fiery Olive and Sunflower Oil with Herbs.

GRILLED LAMB CUBES WITH PAPAYA

500 g/1 lb boneless leg of lamb or shoulder, cut into
    2.5 cm/1 inch cubes

MARINADE
5½ tablespoons olive oil
2   tablespoons red wine vinegar
1   clove garlic, chopped
¾   teaspoon ground cumin
½   teaspoon cayenne pepper
½   teaspoon salt
½   teaspoon freshly ground black pepper
¼   teaspoon ground coriander

TO ASSEMBLE
2   ripe but firm papayas, peeled, seeded and cut into
    2 cm/¾ inch cubes
2   tablespoons fresh lemon juice
30 wooden skewers (15 cm/6 inches long)

Papayas are often picked—and sold— green. Ripen them in a warm, sunny spot until they become more yellow than green and have begun to soften.

Place lamb cubes in a shallow glass or non-reactive dish.

In a small bowl, whisk together oil, vinegar, garlic, cumin, cayenne, salt, black pepper and coriander. Pour marinade over lamb, stirring gently to coat meat well. Set aside at room temperature and let marinate for 2 hours; or chill in the refrigerator for up to 8 hours.

Place skewers in a shallow dish, add enough water to cover and let soak for at least 1 hour before assembling and cooking lamb and papaya.

Build a charcoal fire in a barbecue or preheat grill.

Meanwhile, in a mixing bowl sprinkle papaya cubes with lemon juice and toss gently to coat fruit thoroughly.

Drain skewers. Then thread cubes of marinated lamb and papaya on to each skewer. Brush each lightly with remaining marinade.

When coals have burned down to a moderately hot fire, arrange skewers around edge so that blunt ends are not directly over coals. Cook for 5 to 10 minutes, brushing with marinade and using blunt ends of skewers as handles for turning meat occasionally so that all sides brown equally. Lamb should be nicely browned all over but still pink inside. Arrange attractively on a platter and serve immediately.

— MAKES 30 HORS D'OEUVRES —

QUAIL'S EGGS WRAPPED IN ROASTED PEPPERS

USING GREEN, YELLOW AND RED PEPPERS MAKES THIS A PARTICULARLY colourful presentation when served on a plain white plate. Wrap the eggs in pepper strips several hours in advance, cover lightly and refrigerate. Remove from the refrigerator long enough in advance to warm to room temperature. Then dip eggs in the oil and herbs just before serving.

24   quail's eggs
1   each green, red and yellow peppers
4   tablespoons finely chopped mixed fresh herbs such as parsley, chives, thyme, chervil, dill and marjoram
1   teaspoon salt
2   tablespoons olive or hazelnut oil

Place eggs in a saucepan. Add enough hot water to cover them by about 5 cm/2 inches, bring to the boil and boil for 2 minutes. Drain off water and refresh eggs under cold water to stop the cooking. Let the eggs cool completely.

Meanwhile, roast the peppers. Pierce the stalk end of each pepper with a wooden-handled kitchen fork and hold pepper directly over gas burner, turning slowly, until all sides are well charred. Or place peppers on a baking sheet and grill as close to heat source as possible, turning occasionally, until thoroughly charred. Place peppers in a paper bag and close it tightly to allow peppers to steam for several minutes. Remove from the bag and rinse peppers under cold water, rubbing off blackened skin with the fingers. Halve each pepper lengthways and remove core, seeds and membrane. Cut each lengthways into 1 cm/½ inch wide strips.

Peel the eggs, cracking the shell all over and starting to peel at the blunt end, where there is usually an air pocket that makes the peeling easier. Wrap each egg in a strip of roasted pepper and secure in place with a cocktail stick.

In a small dish, combine herbs and salt and mix well. In another dish, place the oil. Dip half of each pepper-wrapped egg into the oil, then dip in the herb mixture. Arrange on a platter and serve.

— MAKES 24 HORS D'OEUVRES —

Put any extra strips of roasted pepper into a jar and cover them with olive oil. These can be refrigerated for up to 2 weeks and served in salads and rice dishes or with grilled meats. The resulting oil contributes an elusive and delicious flavour to vinaigrettes.

WHITE HAZELNUT FRUITCAKE

AS THIS CAKE HAS A PARTICULARLY FINE TEXTURE AND FLAVOUR AND keeps well, it is a very good one to have on hand during holiday seasons. The cake needs 3 days to mellow, but it can be made 2 weeks ahead and moistened by sprinkling the muslin with a few spoonfuls of rum.

125 g/4 oz dried apricots, coarsely chopped
60 g/2 oz dried pears, coarsely chopped
60 g/2 oz dried figs, coarsely chopped
60 g/2 oz dried pineapple, coarsely chopped
150 g/5 oz sultanas
90 g/3 oz candied citron, chopped
250 ml/8 fl oz dark rum
275 g/9 oz shelled hazelnuts
500 g/1 lb plain flour
2   teaspoons baking powder
1   teaspoon salt
350 g/12 oz unsalted butter, softened
500 g/1 lb caster sugar
7   size 3 eggs, separated
2   teaspoons grated lemon zest
1   teaspoon freshly grated nutmeg
2   teaspoons orange flower water
1   teaspoon vanilla essence

In a mixing bowl, combine apricots, pears, figs, pineapple, sultanas and citron with 150 ml/¼ pint of the rum and set fruit aside to macerate for several hours or overnight.

Preheat oven to 180° C/350° F/Gas 4.

Spread hazelnuts in a single layer on a baking sheet. Bake in centre of hot oven, stirring frequently and watching carefully, for 6 to 8 minutes, or until nuts are toasted and fragrant. Remove nuts from oven, wrap immediately in a clean tea towel and rub vigorously on a work surface to remove skins. Discard skins and chop nuts coarsely. (If the hazelnuts are already skinned, simply roast them for 6 to 8 minutes and coarsely chop.) Add to macerating fruit.

Reduce oven temperature to 160° C/325° F/Gas 3.

Sift flour with baking powder and salt on to a sheet of greaseproof paper and set aside.

In a large mixing bowl, cream together butter and sugar and beat in the egg yolks, one at a time, beating for about 1 minute after each addition, until mixture becomes very light and fluffy. Add lemon zest, nutmeg, orange flower water, vanilla essence and flour mixture and beat until well blended. Stir in fruit, hazelnuts and macerating liquid.

In a very clean large bowl, beat egg whites until stiff but not dry peaks form. Stir about one-quarter of whites into fruitcake batter to lighten, then gently fold in remaining whites. (The batter will be heavy, so it may be easiest to fold whites in with your hands.)

Spoon batter into a 25 cm/10 inch angel cake tin that has been buttered, lined with buttered parchment paper and floured. Smooth top of batter with a spatula. Bake in centre of oven for 1 hour and 10 minutes to 1 hour and 20 minutes, or until cake is a rich golden brown and a skewer inserted into centre comes out clean.

Remove from oven and let cool in tin for 15 minutes. Using a small knife, loosen edges of cake and turn out on to a wire rack to cool completely.

In a bowl, soak in remaining rum a square of muslin large enough to completely wrap cake. Spread the rum-soaked muslin on a large sheet of aluminium foil. Place cake in centre and wrap tightly with the muslin and then with the foil. Put in a cool dry place to mellow for at least 3 days. To serve, remove from the wrappings and slice very thinly.

— MAKES ABOUT 24 THIN SLICES —

The unusual combination of fruits and nuts gives this cake its distinctive taste. Other dried and candied citrus fruits and peels may be used—as well as almonds or walnuts—in your favourite combination, as long as the total quantity is the same as in the recipe.

BLINIS WITH HERBS, SALMON ROE AND SOURED CREAM

BLINIS ARE BEST FRESH, PREPARED JUST BEFORE ASSEMBLING AND serving. But they can also be made in advance, arranged in a single layer on a baking sheet and covered loosely with foil. Reheat for 10 minutes in a 160° C/325° F/Gas 3 oven just before topping with soured cream and salmon roe. They are particularly attractive when served on a silver platter lined with a starched white linen napkin.

These are often made in part or entirely with buckwheat flour; the result is less light but more flavourful. Thin slivers of pickled herring, smoked salmon or smoked trout can be substituted for the salmon roe.

BLINIS
175 ml/6 fl oz milk
45 g/1½ oz unsalted butter
175 g/6 oz plain flour
1½ teaspoons easy-blend dried yeast
1 teaspoon caster sugar
½ teaspoon salt
2 size 3 eggs, separated
2 tablespoons finely chopped fresh chives
2 tablespoons finely chopped fresh parsley
Butter for cooking blinis

TO ASSEMBLE
125 ml/4 fl oz soured cream or *crème fraîche*
125 ml/4 fl oz red salmon roe
Freshly ground pepper
35 flat-leaf parsley leaves

In a small saucepan, heat milk and butter over low heat until butter is almost melted, remove from the heat and set aside to allow butter to finish melting and liquid to cool to lukewarm.

Meanwhile, combine flour, yeast, sugar and salt in a food processor and pulse with on/off motion to blend. With motor running pour milk mixture through feed tube into dry ingredients and pulse to blend. Add egg yolks and pulse until well mixed. Transfer batter into a mixing bowl, cover and set aside in a warm place to rise for about 40 minutes, or until double in bulk.

Heat a griddle or large, heavy frying pan. Beat egg whites until stiff and fold them, along with chives and parsley, into the risen batter.

Butter hot griddle just enough to prevent the blinis from sticking. Drop batter by ½ tablespoons on to griddle, spreading it out if necessary to make 4 cm/1½ inch rounds. Cook each side for about 40 seconds, adjusting heat if necessary so that blinis brown nicely without burning.

To assemble, spread ¾ teaspoon soured cream over the top of each blini. Top with ¾ teaspoon salmon roe and grind a little pepper over the top. Garnish each with a parsley leaf.

— MAKES 35 HORS D'OEUVRES —

DINNER

MIDSUMMER'S NIGHT

MENU

◆

*M*ELON AND PROSCIUTTO SALAD WITH LIME-PEPPER VINAIGRETTE

◆

*M*ARINATED TUNA STEAKS WITH TOMATO-BASIL SAUCE

◆

*B*ABY SQUASH WITH NASTURTIUM BUTTER

◆

*L*EMON RICE

◆

*P*EACH LATTICE PIE

PHOTO: MARINATED SWORDFISH STEAK WITH TOMATO-BASIL SAUCE

MELON AND PROSCIUTTO SALAD WITH LIME-PEPPER VINAIGRETTE

ANY COMBINATION OF THREE RIPE MELONS CAN BE USED, BUT A mixture of colours produces the prettiest salad.

½ rock or Charentais melon
½ honeydew melon
½ Ogen melon

LIME-PEPPER VINAIGRETTE
4 tablespoons fresh lime juice
2 teaspoons honey
1 teaspoon Crabtree & Evelyn Provençal Herbs Mustard or Dijon mustard
½ teaspoon coarsely ground pepper
¼ teaspoon grated lime zest
4 tablespoons walnut oil
4 tablespoons safflower or sunflower oil
Salt

TO ASSEMBLE
2 medium bunches watercress
6 thin slices prosciutto or Westphalian ham

These ingredients also make wonderful summer hors d'oeuvres. Cut the melon into finger-size sticks, lay a sprig of watercress on each and wrap in a slice of prosciutto so that the watercress leaves stick out from one end. Build into triangular piles on a serving platter, with the leafy ends alternately facing front and back.

Scoop out and discard seeds from melon halves and slice each half into neat 5 to 10 mm/¼ to ½ inch thick slices. Trim off rind and discard.

In a mixing bowl, whisk together lime juice, honey, mustard, pepper, and lime zest. Slowly add walnut oil and safflower oil, whisking until dressing is thoroughly blended. Season to taste with salt, according to saltiness of ham.

Snap off and discard tough stalks from watercress, add leaves to dressing, and toss to coat lightly.

Divide watercress salad among 6 large salad plates, arrange slightly overlapping slices of the 3 melons in centres and drape a slice of prosciutto over each serving. Serve immediately.

— 6 SERVINGS —

*B*ABY SQUASH WITH NASTURTIUM BUTTER

IF BABY SQUASH IS NOT AVAILABLE, USE SMALL COURGETTES CUT INTO thick slices.

750 g/1½ lb assorted baby squash such as courgettes
      (green and yellow), mustard marrow, pattypan and
      butternut
90 g/3 oz unsalted butter
2 teaspoons finely chopped shallot
3 tablespoons unsprayed fresh nasturtium leaves,
      rinsed, patted dry, and chopped
3 tablespoons unsprayed fresh nasturtium blossoms,
      rinsed, patted dry, and chopped
1 teaspoon shallot-flavoured white wine vinegar
      Salt
      Freshly ground pepper

TO SERVE
Whole unsprayed fresh nasturtium blossoms and
leaves

The peppery taste of nasturtium leaves lends itself to flavouring vegetables and salads, while the leaves between thin slices of lightly buttered bread make delicate tea sandwiches.

Place squash in a steamer basket set in a large saucepan of 4 to 5 cm/1½ to 2 inches boiling water and steam it for 3 to 6 minutes, or until just tender. (Steaming time will vary with size of squash.)

Meanwhile, melt butter in a medium frying pan, add shallot and sauté until softened, about 3 minutes. Stir in chopped nasturtium leaves and blossoms and vinegar and simmer over low heat, stirring, for about 1 minute. Season with salt and pepper. (Nasturtiums have a peppery taste, so add pepper sparingly.)

Add warm steamed squash to pan and toss gently to coat well with nasturtium butter. To serve, place on a large platter and garnish with whole nasturtium blossoms and leaves.

— 6 SERVINGS —

Marinated Tuna Steaks with Tomato-Basil Sauce

IF FRESH TUNA IS NOT AVAILABLE, SWORDFISH CAN BE SUBSTITUTED, IN which case the cooking time should be increased to 5 to 6 minutes per side, because swordfish is not usually served medium-rare. The sauce can be made a few hours in advance and reheated just before serving.

The tomato-basil sauce can double as a lovely fresh summer pasta sauce, particularly when paired with mushroom-stuffed tortellini.

6	fresh 2.5 cm/1 inch thick tuna steaks (about 175 g/6 oz each)
	Coarsely ground pepper
6	tablespoons olive oil
2	tablespoons fresh lemon juice
2	tablespoons chopped fresh oregano, or 2 teaspoons dried

TOMATO-BASIL SAUCE

25	g/¾ oz unsalted butter
1½	tablespoons olive oil
3	tablespoons finely chopped shallot
2	tablespoons red wine
1	tablespoon sherry vinegar
500	g/1 lb plum tomatoes, peeled, seeded and diced
1½	tablespoons shredded fresh basil leaves
	Salt
	Freshly ground pepper

TO SERVE

6	small sprigs fresh oregano
6	small fresh basil leaves

Sprinkle tuna steaks on both sides with pepper. Combine oil, lemon juice and chopped oregano in a shallow glass or non-reactive dish just large enough to hold tuna steaks in a single layer and stir to blend. Add tuna steaks, turning them to coat both sides with marinade. Set aside at room temperature and let marinate for 1 hour, turning once or twice.

Build a charcoal fire in a barbecue or preheat grill.

Meanwhile, in a medium frying pan melt butter with oil over medium heat, add shallot and cook until softened, about 3 minutes. Add wine and vinegar and reduce over high heat, stirring, for about 1 minute. Reduce heat to medium-low, add tomatoes and simmer for 5 to 6 minutes, or until most of the liquid is evaporated. Stir in shredded basil, season with salt and pepper and simmer for 30 seconds. Keep warm while grilling tuna.

When coals have burned down to medium-hot or when grill is heated, place tuna steaks on grid or grill tray 10 to 12.5 cm/4 to 5 inches from fire and cook each side for about 4 minutes, or until tuna is medium-rare in centre. Season with salt, if desired.

Place tuna steaks on a large platter, spoon sauce over top and garnish each steak with a sprig of oregano and a basil leaf. Serve immediately.

— 6 SERVINGS —

*L*EMON RICE

60 g/2 oz butter
90 g/3 oz celery with some leaves, chopped
45 g/1½ oz spring onion (white and some green), chopped
275 g/9 oz long-grain white rice
550 ml/18 fl oz chicken stock
1½ tablespoons lemon juice
1 tablespoon grated lemon zest
1 teaspoon salt (see Note)
⅛ teaspoon freshly ground pepper
1 small bay leaf

TO SERVE
4 tablespoons finely chopped fresh parsley

In a heavy 2 litre/3½ pint saucepan, melt butter over medium-low heat. Add celery and spring onion and cook until softened, about 5 minutes. Stir in rice and cook, stirring, for 1 to 2 minutes, coating all grains with the butter. Stir in stock, lemon juice, lemon zest, salt, pepper and bay leaf. Bring to the boil, reduce heat to low, cover pan and simmer for 20 to 25 minutes, or until all liquid is absorbed and rice is tender. Remove from heat and let stand, covered, for 5 to 8 minutes.

Discard bay leaf. Add parsley and toss rice lightly with a fork to mix and fluff. Serve hot.

— 6 SERVINGS —

Note: If using stock made from a cube instead of homemade stock, reduce quantity of salt to ½ teaspoon or less.

For an old-fashioned rice pudding with a light, delicate flavour, combine 70 g/2⅓ oz raw rice with 4 tablespoons sugar, three 5 cm/2 inch strips of lemon zest, and 600 ml/1 pint milk in a 1 litre/2 pint ovenproof dish and bake the mixture in a 150° C/300° F/ Gas 2 oven for about 1½ hours, stirring every half hour. The pudding is cooked when the rice is tender and the milk has the consistency of single cream.

PEACH LATTICE PIE

THIS PASTRY DOUGH CAN BE MADE A DAY IN ADVANCE AND REFRIGERATED. Or prepare the pastry up to a week in advance and freeze it. If the pastry is too firm to roll, let it stand at room temperature for several minutes until it is just warm enough to work with. If desired, serve the pie with vanilla ice cream flavoured with a little ground cinnamon.

Crabtree & Evelyn flower waters and 'fruit only' conserves can provide variations for this pie. Give the peaches a light, slightly floral taste and aroma by substituting 1 tablespoon orange flower water or rose-water for the sherry in the filling. These natural extracts from the distillation of orange and rose blossoms were an important ingredient in British cookery from Elizabethan times until the nineteenth century and are now enjoying a deserved revival in modern cooking.

PASTRY
300	g/10 oz plus 2 tablespoons plain flour
1	teaspoon caster sugar
1	teaspoon salt
100	g/3½ oz cold unsalted butter
90	g/3 oz cold lard
1	size 3 egg yolk
1½	teaspoons white wine vinegar

PEACH FILLING
150 to 200	g/5 to 7 oz caster sugar
3	tablespoons cornflour
¼	teaspoon ground mace
¼	teaspoon salt
1.5	kg/3 lb fresh peaches, peeled, stoned and thickly sliced
1	tablespoon fresh lemon juice
1	tablespoon dry sherry

TO ASSEMBLE
2	tablespoons peach or apricot preserve
1	tablespoon double cream
2	teaspoons caster sugar

To prepare pastry dough, combine flour, sugar and salt in a large mixing bowl. Add butter and lard and rub it into flour mixture with your fingertips or a fork until mixture resembles small peas.

In a small bowl, whisk together egg yolk, vinegar and 3 tablespoons iced water until well blended. Sprinkle liquid over flour mixture and toss with a fork just until ingredients are moistened and can be formed into a ball. If mixture seems too dry, add up to 1 tablespoon more iced water by teaspoonsful, until a dough forms. Divide dough into 2 balls, one somewhat larger than the other, flatten balls slightly and wrap each in polythene. Chill in the refrigerator for at least 30 minutes.

Meanwhile, in a large mixing bowl combine sugar, cornflour, mace and salt. Add peaches, lemon juice and sherry and toss gently to coat peaches well.

Preheat oven to 220° C/425° F/Gas 7.

On a lightly floured surface, roll out the larger ball of dough into a 30 cm/12 inch round. Ease dough into a deep 22.5 cm/9 inch pie tin or dish. Brush bottom of dough with preserve. (If preserve is too thick to brush on to dough, thin with a few drops of water or sherry.) Spoon filling into pie shell, distributing it evenly.

Roll smaller pastry ball into a 27.5 cm/11 inch round. Using a sharp knife, cut pastry into 1 cm/½ inch wide strips. (You should have about 14 strips.) Weave pastry strips into a lattice over top of pie by placing a strip at the edge of the pie, then placing a second strip at right angles to the first, and continuing to alternate strips in this manner until pie is covered. Press pastry strips firmly in place at edge of pie and flute or crimp pastry all around rim. Brush lattice and edge of pastry with cream. Sprinkle lattice with sugar. Cover crimped edge of pie loosely with aluminium foil. Bake in lower third of oven for 30 minutes.

Remove foil from edge. Reduce oven temperature to 200° C/400° F/ Gas 6 and continue to bake pie for 15 to 20 minutes, or until pastry is a rich golden brown and filling is bubbly.

— MAKES A 22.5 CM/9 INCH PIE —

You can also omit the lattice top for the pie and make a glossy fruit glaze instead with any of the 'fruit only' conserves. Stir 1 tablespoon cornflour into 1 tablespoon cold water and combine with 1 jar of 'fruit only' conserve. In a small saucepan, heat the mixture gently until it bubbles slightly and loses its cloudiness. Bake the peach pie without the lattice top and let it cool. Then gently spread the thickened compote over the filling. Let the pie and glaze cool and serve with lightly whipped cream.

HARVEST MOON

MENU

◆

*T*OMATO AND CELERY
SOUP

◆

*G*LAZED PORK LOIN
WITH GARLIC POTATOES

◆

*B*RUSSELS SPROUTS IN
BROWN BUTTER

◆

*A*PPLE-QUINCE BREAD
PUDDING

OPPOSITE: GLAZED PORK LOIN WITH
GARLIC POTATOES

TOMATO AND CELERY SOUP

THIS FRESH-FLAVOURED SOUP MAKES A LIGHT, COLOURFUL FIRST course for a substantial dinner.

70   g/2¼ oz butter
3   large sticks of celery, with leaves, coarsely diced
1.7 kg/3¾ lb fresh tomatoes, unpeeled, halved and
     seeded
1.1 litres/scant 2 pints chicken stock
150 ml/¼ pint dry white wine
1   bay leaf
1½   tablespoons finely chopped fresh marjoram leaves,
     or ¾ teaspoon dried
¾   teaspoon celery seed
¼   teaspoon caster sugar
4   sprigs fresh parsley
¾   teaspoon Worcestershire sauce
3   dashes Tabasco sauce
     Salt
     Freshly ground black pepper

TO SERVE
Fresh celery leaves

This combination, as delicious cold as hot, becomes a textured aspic when gelatine is added. Soften 15 g/½ oz powdered gelatine (about 2 tablespoons total) in 125 ml/4 fl oz cold water and stir the mixture into the hot soup. Pour the soup mixture into an oiled 2 litre/3½ pint mould and let it cool. Chill the mixture until it is set. Turn the aspic out on to a decorative dish. If using a ring mould, fill the centre with a poultry, fish or rice salad or a bunch of watercress sprigs; if moulded into a solid shape, surround with the salad.

In a 4 litre/7 pint heavy, non-reactive saucepan, melt the butter, add celery and cook over medium-low heat for about 4 minutes, or until celery is softened but not browned. Add tomatoes, stock, wine, bay leaf, marjoram, celery seed, sugar and parsley. Stir well and bring to the boil. Lower heat and simmer gently, uncovered, for 15 to 20 minutes, or until the celery is very soft. Stir in Worcestershire sauce and Tabasco, discard bay leaf and let soup cool slightly.

Turn soup into a food processor and process with on/off motion until soup is a coarse purée with bite-size pieces of celery and tomato still visible. Season to taste with salt and pepper. Return soup to the saucepan and simmer over medium heat until hot. Ladle into individual soup bowls and garnish each serving with celery leaves. Or transfer to a large tureen, sprinkle soup with celery leaves and serve.

— 6 SERVINGS —

APPLE-QUINCE BREAD PUDDING

IF QUINCES ARE NOT AVAILABLE, SUBSTITUTE A SECOND APPLE.

10	to 12 slices day-old firm white bread, crusts removed
4	size 3 eggs
500	ml/16 fl oz double cream
125	ml/4 fl oz milk
90	g/3 oz honey
2	teaspoons vanilla essence
1	large Golden Delicious apple
1	ripe quince
5	tablespoons caster sugar
1½	teaspoons fresh lemon juice

TO SERVE
Crabtree & Evelyn Honey & Ginger Sauce
(optional)

Cut bread into 2.5 cm/1 inch cubes.

In a large mixing bowl, beat eggs lightly. Beat in cream, milk, honey and vanilla essence. Add bread cubes and stir gently. Cover loosely and set aside to soak for 1 to 2 hours.

Preheat oven to 160° C/325° F/Gas 3.

Peel, core and thinly slice apple and quince. In a small mixing bowl, combine fruit with 4 tablespoons of the sugar and the lemon juice and toss until fruit is coated. Fold fruit into soaked bread, turning gently with a spatula until combined.

Spoon mixture into a lightly buttered, shallow 2 litre/3½ pint flame-proof baking dish and smooth top with a spatula. Bake in the centre of oven for 35 minutes.

Sprinkle top of pudding with remaining 1 tablespoon sugar and continue baking for about 10 minutes, or until top of pudding is golden brown and a knife inserted 5 cm/2 inches from the edge comes out clean. (The centre of the pudding will still be slightly runny; it will finish cooking after being removed from oven.) If top of pudding has not formed a golden brown crust, place pudding under preheated grill for 30 to 60 seconds, or until browned.

Serve warm, accompanied by Honey & Ginger Sauce if desired. Or prepare up to 2 hours ahead and serve tepid.

This can also be served with a purée made by stewing dried apricots in water to cover, then blending the apricots in a food processor with enough of the juices to give the consistency of double cream. Sharpen the flavour with a spoonful or so of kirsch, if desired.

— 6 SERVINGS —

GLAZED PORK LOIN WITH GARLIC POTATOES

MEAT AND POTATOES ROASTED TOGETHER ARE ALWAYS DELICIOUS. IN this recipe, the two main ingredients are given their own individual seasoning during the last half hour of cooking: a mustard glaze for the pork loin and garlic for the potatoes. Crabtree & Evelyn Cumberland Sauce may be used in place of the redcurrant jelly.

1	joint pork loin (about 2.3 kg/5 lb), chine bone removed or sawn through to facilitate carving and meat tied at intervals with string
	Salt
	Freshly ground pepper
18	small new red potatoes
3	tablespoons redcurrant jelly
2	teaspoons finely chopped fresh rosemary, or ¾ teaspoon dried
175	ml/6 fl oz dry white wine
2	to 3 teaspoons Champagne-flavoured or Dijon mustard
1	clove garlic, chopped

TO SERVE
Fresh rosemary sprigs

Preheat oven to 160° C/325° F/Gas 3.

Sprinkle pork loin with salt and pepper and place on a rack in a shallow roasting pan. Roast in the centre of the oven for 2 to 2½ hours (about 25 to 30 minutes for each 500 g/1 lb), or until a meat thermometer inserted into the centre of the joint registers 74° C/165° F.

Bring a large saucepan of lightly salted water to the boil. If potatoes are very small, leave them whole and peel away a thin band of skin around the middle of each. If using larger potatoes, do not peel, but cut into 5 cm/2 inch cubes. Cook in boiling water until almost tender, about 10 minutes, and drain thoroughly in a colander.

When joint has cooked for about 1 hour, add potatoes to the roasting pan, turning them in the pan juices to coat well. Turn potatoes occasionally during roasting so that they brown evenly.

In a small saucepan, combine jelly, rosemary and 2 tablespoons of the wine and warm over low heat until the jelly melts. Stir in mustard.

EXTRA JELLY

RED-CURRANT JELLY

PRESERVE

with Cockburns

PORT

About ½ hour before joint is finished cooking, brush glaze over pork. Brush with glaze every 10 minutes.

About 10 minutes before roast has finished cooking, sprinkle garlic over the potatoes.

When the internal temperature of the joint has reached the correct temperature, remove it to a cutting board and allow it to rest for 15 minutes before carving. Remove potatoes from the roasting pan and keep warm.

Skim fat from the juices in the roasting pan. Stir in remaining wine and boil sauce on top of stove for 2 or 3 minutes.

Carve meat downwards next to the bone (if it has not been removed) and arrange slices on a serving platter. Surround with the potatoes and garnish with rosemary sprigs. Serve the sauce separately.

— 6 SERVINGS —

$\mathscr{B}$RUSSELS SPROUTS IN BROWN BUTTER

THE BUTTER CAN BE BROWNED IN ADVANCE AND REHEATED WHEN THE sprouts are draining.

    1   kg/2 lb fresh Brussels sprouts (35 to 40)
    90 g/3 oz unsalted butter
    1   tablespoon fresh lemon juice
        Salt
        Freshly ground pepper

Discard tough and damaged outer leaves from sprouts. Trim away fibrous ends of stalks, being careful not to cut away too much.

Bring a large pan of lightly salted water to the boil over high heat, add sprouts, boil for 7 to 8 minutes, or until just tender, and drain.

Meanwhile, in a large saucepan melt butter over medium heat and cook until it turns a deep golden brown, 3 to 4 minutes, being very careful not to let it burn.

Add Brussels sprouts along with lemon juice to saucepan and toss gently in the brown butter. Season with salt and a generous grinding of pepper, toss well and serve.

— 6 SERVINGS —

Elevate Brussels sprouts into an even more elegant vegetable by purée-ing them. In a food processor, purée the boiled, drained sprouts to a coarse consistency. Stir in the butter and lemon juice and add 4 table-spoons single cream to smooth the consistency slightly. Reheat before serving and sprinkle with a little crumbled cooked bacon.

CHRISTMAS FEAST

MENU

◆

*O*YSTERS GLAZED WITH GREEN PEPPERCORN BUTTER

◆

*R*OAST GOOSE WITH FRUIT AND NUT STUFFING

◆

*C*RANBERRY-PORT SAUCE

◆

A MÉLANGE OF VEGETABLES

◆

*P*OTATO AND PARSNIP PURÉE

◆

*C*HRISTMAS PUDDING WITH NUTMEG HARD SAUCE

OPPOSITE: ROAST GOOSE WITH FRUIT AND NUT STUFFING AND CRANBERRY-PORT SAUCE, A MÉLANGE OF VEGETABLES, AND POTATO AND PARSNIP PURÉE

*O*YSTERS GLAZED WITH GREEN PEPPERCORN BUTTER

THIS MAKES A LIGHT BUT ELEGANT STARTER FOR CHRISTMAS DINNER. The peppercorn butter can be made a couple of days ahead and kept in the refrigerator or frozen earlier still. Bring it to room temperature before using.

2	dozen fresh oysters in the shells
	Coarse salt
45	g/1½ oz fresh breadcrumbs made from day-old bread

GREEN PEPPERCORN BUTTER

125	g/4 oz unsalted butter, softened
2	tablespoons chopped fresh parsley
1	tablespoon chopped shallot
1	tablespoon fresh lemon juice
1	teaspoon crushed dried green peppercorns
	Pinch cayenne pepper
¼	teaspoon salt
	Freshly ground black pepper

Combine butter, parsley, shallot, lemon juice, peppercorns, cayenne, salt and black pepper in a food processor, blender or large mixing bowl and blend or beat together. Taste for seasoning and add more salt if necessary.

Preheat grill.

Open oysters, discarding top half of each shell. Loosen each from bottom half of shell, wiping away any sand or grit, and replace on bottom half of shell. Spread a generous layer of coarse salt over a baking sheet, an ovenproof serving platter or individual ovenproof plates. Arrange oysters on coarse salt.

Spread about 1½ teaspoons green peppercorn butter over top of each oyster, then sprinkle each with 1½ teaspoons breadcrumbs. Grill oysters about 10 cm/4 inches from the heat for about 3 minutes, or until butter is sizzling, crumbs are golden and oysters are plumped and beginning to curl around edges. Serve hot.

— 6 FIRST-COURSE SERVINGS —

A MÉLANGE OF VEGETABLES

EARLY IN THE DAY, SLICE THE CABBAGE AND COVER IT WITH WATER acidulated with 2 teaspoons vinegar or fresh lemon juice to hold the colour. (Before the final cooking, drain the cabbage well and shake it in a clean tea towel until almost dry.) The carrots and beans can be steamed ahead of time, too. The dish should be completed just before serving, but the cooking time is only about 5 minutes.

This recipe provides generous servings, and any that is left over is delicious reheated.

350 g/12 oz carrots, scraped and thinly sliced
    diagonally
500 g/1 lb French beans, trimmed and sliced diagonally
    into 5 cm/2 inch lengths
125 g/4 oz unsalted butter
2   tablespoons herb-flavoured white wine vinegar or
    sherry vinegar
½   small red cabbage (about 350 g/12 oz), thinly
    sliced
1   tablespoon Crabtree & Evelyn Provençal Herbs
    Mustard or Dijon mustard
    Salt
    Freshly ground pepper

Steam carrots and beans in a steamer basket over a pan of boiling water for about 2 minutes, or until crisp-tender. Refresh under cold water to stop cooking and set colour.

Melt butter in a large frying pan over medium-low heat until it foams. When foam subsides, stir in vinegar. Add cabbage and toss over medium-high heat for about 2 minutes, or until it is crisp-tender.

Stir in mustard, carrots and beans and sauté, tossing, until all vegetables are hot, about 1 minute. Season with salt and pepper. Serve immediately.

— 8 SERVINGS —

ROAST GOOSE WITH FRUIT AND NUT STUFFING

GOOSE HAS A LONG TRADITION AS A CHRISTMAS ROAST, AND A FREE-range one is much sought after for the flavour and quality of its meat. It is hardly the meatiest of birds, but as the carcass makes a very fine stock and the fat an excellent frying medium, goose contributes to several meals of good eating.

The day before, the stuffing can be nearly completed, the goose cleaned, and the giblet stock for the gravy prepared, leaving only the final assembly and roasting to be done on Christmas Day.

1	fresh 4.5 to 5.4 kg/10 to 12 lb goose
½	lemon
	Salt
	Freshly ground pepper
	Fruit and Nut Stuffing (page 208)
250	ml/8 fl oz dry red wine
4	black peppercorns
2	sprigs fresh parsley
½	stick of celery, sliced
1	small onion, coarsely chopped
1	bay leaf
3	tablespoons dry Madeira or medium sherry
	Cranberry-Port Sauce (opposite)

The fruit and nut stuffing may be modified and is delicious in a turkey of the same size as the goose. Increase the quantity of butter to 175 g/ 6 oz and cook 250 g/ 8 oz diced smoked or unsmoked streaky bacon with the onions and celery to introduce a rich moistness that counteracts the relative dryness of the turkey.

Remove giblets and neck from goose cavity and set aside. Rinse cavity and skin of goose and pat dry. Rub goose skin with cut side of lemon half. Season inside and out with salt and pepper. Prick goose skin all over without piercing the meat.

Preheat oven to 220° C/425° F/Gas 7.

Stuff goose cavity loosely with fruit and nut stuffing. Turn goose and loosely stuff neck. Securely truss cavity and neck and roast goose, breast side up, on a rack in a shallow roasting pan in centre of oven for 20 minutes. Reduce oven temperature to 180° C/350° F/Gas 4, turn goose breast side down, and continue roasting for 1 hour. Use a baster or spoon to remove excess fat from roasting pan about 3 times during roasting. Turn goose breast side up again and continue roasting for 1 hour, or until meat thermometer inserted into breast registers 79° C/ 175° F. Increase oven temperature to 230° C/450° F/Gas 8 and roast 20 minutes more to crisp skin.

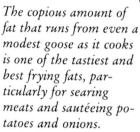

While goose is roasting, in a large saucepan combine giblets and neck with 1 litre/1¾ pints water, half the wine, the peppercorns, parsley, celery, onion and bay leaf, partially cover and simmer over low heat for 1½ to 2 hours, or until liquid is reduced to about 350 ml/12 fl oz. Strain stock into a bowl.

Transfer goose to a warmed carving platter and let it rest for about 15 minutes before carving. Meanwhile, pour off excess fat from roasting pan. Add Madeira to pan juices, scraping up brown bits, stir in goose stock and remaining wine and simmer in roasting pan over low heat for about 10 minutes, or until reduced to about 350 ml/12 fl oz. Season with salt and pepper.

Remove stuffing from goose and place in a serving dish. Carve goose and serve, accompanied by stuffing and Cranberry-Port Sauce.

— 6 TO 8 SERVINGS —

CRANBERRY-PORT SAUCE

THIS SAUCE CAN BE MADE A FEW DAYS IN ADVANCE AND STORED IN THE refrigerator. Bring to room temperature before serving.

```
500  g/1 lb fresh cranberries
175  ml/6 fl oz port
100  g/3½ oz caster sugar
  4  tablespoons orange juice
  1  tablespoon grated orange zest
     a 5 mm/¼ inch thick slice of fresh root ginger
  2  tablespoons redcurrant jelly
```

In a large enamel or other non-reactive saucepan, combine cranberries, port, sugar, orange juice, orange zest and root ginger. Bring to the boil over medium-high heat, stirring to dissolve sugar. Reduce heat to low and simmer for 12 to 15 minutes, stirring frequently, until cranberries have popped and the sauce is slightly thickened. Discard ginger, stir in jelly and set aside to cool. Serve at room temperature with roast poultry.

— MAKES ABOUT 750 ML/1¼ PINTS —

The copious amount of fat that runs from even a modest goose as it cooks is one of the tastiest and best frying fats, particularly for searing meats and sautéeing potatoes and onions.

To keep it, heat the fat until liquid, then strain it through several thicknesses of muslin into jars. Covered and refrigerated, it will keep well for several months.

A flavourful sauce can also be made simply by combining 1 tablespoon grated orange zest, 1 teaspoon freshly grated root ginger and 1 or 2 teaspoons port with a jar of Crabtree & Evelyn Wild Cranberry Sauce.

FRUIT AND NUT STUFFING

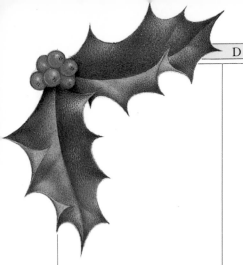

60 g/2 oz stoned dried prunes, quartered
60 g/2 oz dried apricots, quartered
4 tablespoons Madeira or medium sherry
60 g/2 oz shelled walnuts, coarsely broken
60 g/2 oz blanched almonds, coarsely chopped
30 g/1 oz butter
1 large onion, chopped
1 stick of celery, chopped
1 tart apple, peeled, cored and coarsely chopped
1 firm ripe pear, peeled, cored and coarsely chopped
60 g/2 oz fresh kumquats, including skin, seeded and
    coarsely chopped (see Note)
4 tablespoons chopped fresh parsley
1 teaspoon grated orange zest
1 teaspoon dried sage
½ teaspoon dried thyme
⅛ teaspoon ground cinnamon
¼ teaspoon ground mace
    Pinch ground coriander
1 teaspoon salt
¼ teaspoon freshly ground pepper
90 g/3 oz day-old wholemeal bread, cubed

This can be prepared a day ahead to the point of adding the bread cubes and macerated fruit, nuts and lightly cooked ingredients.

The night before assembling stuffing, combine prunes, apricots and Madeira in a bowl and let fruit macerate overnight.

The next day, preheat oven to 180° C/350° F/Gas 4.

Spread walnuts and almonds on a baking sheet and toast in oven for 5 to 10 minutes, or until lightly browned and fragrant.

Melt butter in a large frying pan. Add onion and celery and cook over low heat for about 2 minutes. Add apple and pear and cook for about 3 minutes more, or until vegetables and fruit are softened. Remove pan from heat and stir in kumquats, parsley, orange zest, sage, thyme, cinnamon, mace, coriander, salt and pepper. Add bread cubes, macerated dried fruit with its liquid and toasted nuts and toss to mix well.

— MAKES ENOUGH TO STUFF A 4.5 TO 5.4 KG/10 TO 12 LB BIRD —

Note: If kumquats are unavailable, substitute Crabtree & Evelyn Orange Fruit Only Conserve or Black Currant Fruit Only Conserve.

POTATO AND PARSNIP PURÉE

TO SIMPLIFY THE COOKING ON CHRISTMAS DAY, THE POTATOES AND parsnips can be peeled and cut, ready for cooking, the day before. Put them in bowls or saucepans and cover with cold water.

1   kg/2 lb potatoes, peeled and quartered
350 g/12 oz parsnips, peeled and cut into large pieces
125 g/4 oz butter
60 g/2 oz spring onions (white and some green),
      finely chopped
125 to 250 ml/4 to 8 fl oz milk, heated
      Salt
      Freshly ground pepper
2   tablespoons chopped fresh parsley
2   tablespoons chopped fresh chives

TO SERVE
Several chive blades

Bring a large pan of lightly salted water to the boil over high heat, add potatoes and boil for 10 minutes. Add parsnips and boil for 10 minutes more, or until parsnips and potatoes are tender.

Meanwhile, melt butter in a small saucepan over low heat. Add spring onions and cook over medium-low heat until softened, about 2 minutes.

Drain potatoes and parsnips, return them to pan, and heat for about 1 minute, tossing to let all excess moisture evaporate.

Pass potatoes and parsnips through a food mill, or mash with a masher. Slowly stir in 125 ml/4 fl oz milk and blend well. If too thick, add additional milk. Beat in spring onion mixture, season with salt and pepper, and blend in parsley and chopped chives.

To serve, spoon mixture into a serving dish and arrange 5 cm/2 inch lengths of chive blades in a fan shape on top.

— 8 SERVINGS —

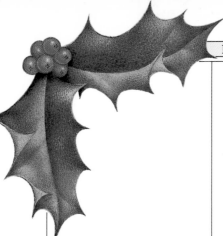

CHRISTMAS PUDDING WITH NUTMEG HARD SAUCE

THESE PUDDINGS ARE ALWAYS BEST WHEN MADE SEVERAL WEEKS ahead—at least—to allow the flavour to develop. Wrap the steamed pudding in brandy-soaked muslin and foil and store it in a cool, dry place. To reheat it, remove the foil and muslin, place the pudding back in its basin and steam for about 1 hour. Or rewrap it in foil and warm it in a low oven for about 45 minutes.

70	g/2½ oz plain flour
1	teaspoon ground cinnamon
½	teaspoon bicarbonate of soda
½	teaspoon salt
¼	teaspoon ground cloves
¼	teaspoon grated nutmeg
¼	teaspoon ground mace
125	g/4 oz minced fresh ground beef suet (kidney fat)
150	g/5 oz light brown sugar
3	size 3 eggs
3	tablespoons plum preserve
1	tablespoon grated orange zest
75	g/2½ oz dry breadcrumbs
125	g/4 oz dried figs, chopped
125	g/4 oz shelled pecan nuts, coarsely chopped
90	g/3 oz stoned dates, chopped
45	g/1½ oz currants
45	g/1½ oz raisins
45	g/1½ oz sultanas
45	g/1½ oz candied citron, chopped
45	g/1½ oz candied orange peel, chopped
45	g/1½ oz candied lemon peel, chopped
30	g/1 oz crystallized ginger, chopped
	Nutmeg Hard Sauce (recipe follows)

Sift together flour, cinnamon, bicarbonate of soda, salt, cloves, nutmeg and mace on to a sheet of greaseproof paper.

In a large mixing bowl, beat suet until as creamy as possible. Add brown sugar and beat thoroughly. Add eggs, one at a time, beating well

after each addition. (Mixture may look curdled at this point.) Beat in plum preserve and orange zest. Add flour mixture and breadcrumbs and beat until well blended. Stir in figs, pecans, dates, currants, raisins, sultanas, citron, orange peel, lemon peel and ginger.

Spoon batter into a 2 litre/3½ pint pudding basin that has been well buttered and sprinkled lightly with caster sugar. Cover basin tightly with lid, or with pleated greaseproof paper and foil tied with string, and set on a wire rack in a large pan. Pour in enough boiling water to come about halfway up side of pudding basin. Cover pan tightly and steam pudding over very low heat for 3½ to 4½ hours, or until a skewer inserted into the centre of pudding comes out clean.

Remove pudding basin from pan and let pudding cool 10 minutes in the basin. Carefully turn out pudding and wrap in brandy-soaked muslin and foil and store in a cool, dry place. When ready to serve, reheat and serve with Nutmeg Hard Sauce.

— 8 TO 10 SERVINGS —

$\mathcal{N}$UTMEG HARD SAUCE

THIS SAUCE CAN BE MADE A FEW DAYS AHEAD AND STORED IN THE refrigerator. Bring to room temperature before serving, and, if necessary, beat sauce briefly to return it to a light, fluffy consistency.

125 g/4 oz unsalted butter, softened
90 g/3 oz icing sugar
¼ cup Cognac or other brandy
½ teaspoon freshly grated nutmeg
½ teaspoon vanilla essence
Pinch salt
2 tablespoons double cream

TO SERVE
Freshly grated nutmeg

In a mixing bowl, cream together butter and sugar until very light and fluffy. Add Cognac, nutmeg, vanilla essence and salt and beat until very light. If sauce seems too stiff, slowly add the cream until light and fluffy.

Spoon sauce into a small serving dish and grate a little nutmeg over top. Serve with Christmas pudding.

— MAKES 175 ML/6 FL OZ —

For a highly effective, deceptively easy Christmas dessert, crumble leftover pudding (or a whole small pudding) and fold it into high-quality bought or home-made vanilla ice cream. A tablespoonful of brandy will also enhance the flavour.

DINNER FOR A
FAVOURITE UNCLE

M E N U

◆

*F*OIE GRAS SALAD WITH
COGNAC VINAIGRETTE

◆

*B*RAISED VEAL WITH
COARSE-GRAINED
MUSTARD SAUCE

◆

*P*URÉE OF BROCCOLI
AND PEAS

◆

*W*ILD RICE AND GRAPES

◆

*C*HOCOLATE ALMOND
CAKE WITH RUM CREAM

OPPOSITE: CHOCOLATE ALMOND CAKE
WITH RUM CREAM

$\mathcal{F}$OIE GRAS SALAD WITH COGNAC VINAIGRETTE

THE COGNAC VINAIGRETTE MAY BE PREPARED IN ADVANCE AND RE-frigerated until needed. Bring to room temperature and whisk to blend just before serving. The salads may be assembled ahead up to the point of adding the *foie gras* and dressing and refrigerated until serving time.

Freshly sautéed duck livers make a handsome alternative to the foie gras. *Clean and trim 3 duck livers, season them with salt and pepper, and sauté them in butter over medium-high heat for about 3 minutes, or until they are cooked outside and pink and juicy in the centre. Let the livers cool to room temperature. When assembling the salad, cut the livers in thin, diagonal slices and arrange them on the greens.*

COGNAC VINAIGRETTE

2	tablespoons olive oil
2	shallots, finely chopped
3	tablespoons Cognac or other brandy
3	tablespoons red wine vinegar
1	teaspoon Dijon mustard
150	ml/¼ pint vegetable oil
1	tablespoon walnut oil
¾	teaspoon salt
⅛	teaspoon freshly ground pepper

SALAD

30	*haricots verts* (French beans) or pencil-thin asparagus spears
1	small head endive, torn into pieces
1	bunch rocket, tough ends trimmed
½	red pepper, cored, seeded and cut into thin strips
60	g/2 oz fresh or canned cooked *foie gras*

In a small frying pan, combine olive oil and shallots and cook over medium heat for 1 minute. Remove pan from heat, add Cognac and let it warm in the hot pan for a few seconds. Carefully light Cognac with a match and allow the alcohol to burn off, gently shaking pan until flames die out. Pour shallot mixture into a mixing bowl and allow to cool slightly. Add vinegar and mustard and whisk to blend. Gradually whisk in vegetable and walnut oils until a thick vinaigrette forms. Add salt and pepper and whisk to blend.

Top and tail beans. If using asparagus, trim off all but 6 cm/2½ inches of tips, reserving the remaining portion of spears for another use. Plunge beans or asparagus tips into a large saucepan of rapidly boiling water and blanch for 2 minutes. Drain in a colander, refresh under cold water to stop cooking and drain again.

Divide endive and rocket leaves among 6 individual salad plates. Arrange beans or asparagus and red pepper over greens.

Just before serving, cut the *foie gras* into 6 thin slices and place one slice in the centre of each salad. Drizzle about 2 tablespoons Cognac vinaigrette over each serving.

Serve immediately.

— 6 SERVINGS —

WILD RICE AND GRAPES

THIS IS AN ESPECIALLY GOOD COMBINATION; BUT, IF WILD RICE IS unavailable, natural brown rice may be used instead.

250 g/8 oz wild rice
60 g/2 oz butter
90 g/3 oz onion, chopped
1   teaspoon salt
20 seedless green grapes, halved
20 purple grapes, halved and, if necessary, pipped
4   tablespoon finely chopped fresh parsley
      Freshly ground pepper

Rinse the rice thoroughly in a colander and let drain.

In a large heavy saucepan or frying pan with a lid, melt 45 g/1½ oz of the butter. Add onion and cook over low heat for 3 to 4 minutes, or until softened. Add rice and toss to coat with butter. Stir in 750 ml/1¼ pints water and the salt. Bring to a simmer, cover tightly and cook over low heat, stirring occasionally, for 45 to 50 minutes, or until rice is tender and all water is absorbed. If water is absorbed before rice is tender, add a few tablespoons more and continue cooking.

Melt the remaining butter in a medium frying pan. Add green and purple grapes and toss in the butter until heated through. Add grape mixture and parsley to the cooked wild rice, season with pepper and toss to mix thoroughly. Add additional salt if necessary. Serve hot.

— 6 GENEROUS SERVINGS —

$\mathscr{B}$RAISED VEAL WITH
COARSE-GRAINED MUSTARD SAUCE

ASK THE BUTCHER TO SAVE THE BONES FROM THE VEAL LOIN AND TIE them to the bottom of loin to act as a rack during braising and to flavour the sauce. Or ask for about 1 kg/2 lb small veal bones and simply add them to the roasting pan to cook with veal loin.

A joint of pork loin could be used in place of the veal, but the cooking time should then be increased by half an hour. The full-bodied but not overwhelming sauce is a fine foil to the delicate taste of the meat.

1	joint boneless loin of veal (1.4 kg/3 lb), tied with string, plus about 1 kg/2 lb veal bones
	Salt
	Freshly ground pepper
45	g/1½ oz plus 20 g/⅔ oz butter
3	tablespoons vegetable oil
60	g/2 oz carrot, finely diced
60	g/2 oz celery, finely diced
45	g/1½ oz leek, finely diced
125	g/4 oz onion, finely diced
4	tablespoons port
350	ml/12 fl oz dry white wine
1	bouquet garni composed of 1 parsley sprig, 1 bay leaf, ¼ teaspoon dried marjoram, 1 teaspoon dried rosemary and ¼ teaspoon dried thyme, all tied together in a square of muslin
4	teaspoons plain flour
2	teaspoons coarse-grained mustard

Pat veal joint dry and season lightly with salt and pepper. Place 20 g/⅔ oz of the butter in a small bowl and reserve to soften.

Preheat oven to 190° C/375° F/Gas 5.

In a large frying pan, melt 15 g/½ oz of the remaining butter with 1 tablespoon oil. Add carrot, celery, leek and onion and cook over low heat until softened, about 10 minutes. Using a slotted spoon, transfer vegetables to a roasting pan or ovenproof casserole.

In the frying pan, melt the 30 g/1 oz remaining butter with the 2 remaining tablespoons oil. Add veal joint and brown over medium-high heat until well-browned on all sides. Place meat on bed of cooked vegetables in roasting pan.

Pour port into frying pan and reduce over medium-high heat to about 2 tablespoons, scraping up any brown bits. Pour port mixture over veal. Add wine, bouquet garni and 350 ml/12 fl oz water. (If veal bones were not tied to the loin, add them to the roasting pan at this point.)

Cover roasting pan tightly with a lid or heavy-duty aluminium foil. Place in the centre of oven and immediately reduce oven temperature to 160° C/325° F/Gas 3. Cook for 1¼ to 1½ hours (about 30 minutes for each 500 g/1 lb), or until a meat thermometer inserted in centre of meat registers 79° C/175° F.

Discard bones and bouquet garni. Transfer meat to a serving platter and keep warm while preparing sauce.

Pour juices from roasting pan into a large saucepan, skim off fat and bring juices to a simmer. Cook over high heat, skimming off fat and particles that rise to the surface, until sauce is reduced and thickened slightly, about 10 minutes.

Meanwhile, blend flour and mustard into the reserved softened butter. Whisk this *beurre manié*, ½ teaspoon at a time, into the sauce and simmer for 3 to 4 minutes more to cook flour completely and thicken sauce. Taste and season, if necessary, with salt and pepper.

Remove trussing strings from meat and slice into 1 cm/½ inch thick slices. Spoon some of the sauce over meat slices. Serve remaining sauce in a sauce boat.

— 6 SERVINGS —

Any leftover veal can be thinly sliced and served at room temperature with a simple tuna mayonnaise for a quickly made version of the classic vitello tonnato. For about 350 ml/12 fl oz tuna mayonnaise combine a 90 g/3 oz can tuna, drained, in a food processor or blender with 250 ml/8 fl oz good-quality mayonnaise, 3 flat anchovy fillets, and 3 tablespoons cream. Blend the mixture until smooth, thinning it to the consistency of single cream with a few spoonfuls dry white wine, and then season to taste with lemon juice and cayenne. Arrange the sliced veal on a serving dish, spoon the sauce over it, and sprinkle 2 tablespoons drained capers on top. Cover with cling film and let marinate in the refrigerator for a couple of hours. Bring the sauced veal back to room temperature before serving.

PURÉE OF BROCCOLI AND PEAS

Although the food processor allows every cook to make vegetable purées as smooth as cream in a matter of seconds, those with a bit of texture remaining are often more interesting.

THE PURÉE CAN BE MADE EARLY IN THE DAY AND REHEATED JUST before serving. Leftovers may be heated in good-quality clear stock or broth to make an attractive and tasty soup.

1	large bunch broccoli (about 1 kg/2 lb)
300	g/10 oz frozen peas
90	g/3 oz butter
4	tablespoons double cream
½	teaspoon salt
⅛	teaspoon freshly ground pepper
	Pinch freshly grated nutmeg

Trim off and discard tough ends of broccoli and cut broccoli into 2.5 cm/1 inch pieces. Bring a large saucepan or stockpot of lightly salted water to the boil, add broccoli and boil until almost tender, about 8 minutes. Add peas and boil with broccoli another 4 to 5 minutes, or until both vegetables are tender. Drain vegetables in a colander.

While vegetables are still warm, purée them (in 2 batches if necessary) in a food processor with the butter and cream, using an on/off motion, until mixture is smooth but retains textured flecks of each vegetable. Return purée to saucepan, season with salt, pepper and nutmeg and stir to blend. Warm gently over low heat and serve.

— 6 SERVINGS —

CHOCOLATE ALMOND CAKE WITH RUM CREAM

TAKE CARE NOT TO OVERCOOK THIS LOVELY, ULTRA-MOIST CHOCOlate cake. It is best slightly underdone in the centre, and since it contains no raw flour to upset the taste or digestion there's no danger in serving it a little undercooked. It can be made early in the day or a day in advance. Substitute 250 g/8 oz good marmalade for the icing sugar and rum in the cream for a different flavour.

175 g/6 oz plain chocolate, broken into chunks
90   g/3 oz unsalted butter
4   tablespoons caster sugar
3   size 3 eggs, separated
45   g/1½ oz plus 2 tablespoons ground almonds
45   g/1½ oz fine fresh breadcrumbs

RUM CREAM
175 ml/6 fl oz double cream
      Icing sugar, to taste
4   tablespoons dark rum

Preheat oven to 190° C/375° F/Gas 5.

In a medium saucepan, heat chocolate and butter over very low heat until both are melted. Remove from heat and stir in sugar and egg yolks. Stir in 45 g/1½ oz of the ground almonds and the breadcrumbs.

In a separate bowl, beat egg whites until stiff but not dry. Spoon about a quarter of the chocolate mixture into the whites and fold gently together. Pour in remaining chocolate mixture and fold in lightly but thoroughly.

Turn batter into a 20 cm/8 inch springform cake tin that has been buttered and dusted with the remaining 2 tablespoons ground almonds. Bake in the centre of oven for 25 minutes, or until almost, but not quite, set in the middle. Let cool in the tin on a wire rack. (The cake will deflate slightly.)

To make the sauce, whip the cream until stiff peaks form. Sweeten to taste with icing sugar, then stir in the rum. Whip briefly to re-thicken cream and serve in a bowl with the cake, or pipe cream decoratively on top of the cake.

— 6 TO 8 SERVINGS —

SUPPER

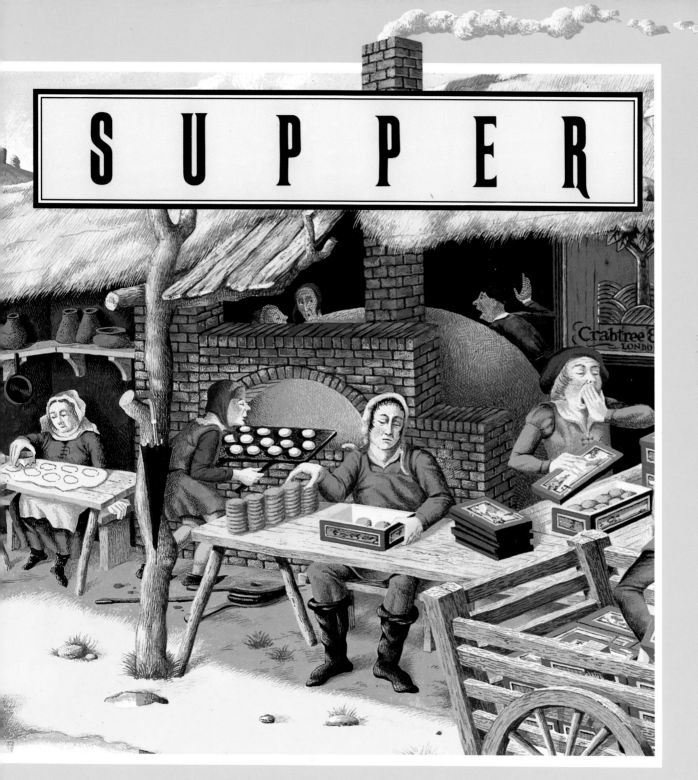

WARM SUMMER'S EVENING

MENU

◆

PRAWN AND MANGE-TOUT PAELLA

◆

BRIE AND BLUEBERRY SALAD

◆

GRUYÈRE ROLLS
(PAGE 246)

◆

MOLASSES-RUM LACE WAFERS

◆

LIME ICE WITH CANDIED LIME ZEST

OPPOSITE: BRIE AND BLUEBERRY SALAD,
PRAWN AND MANGE-TOUT PAELLA,
LIME ICE WITH CANDIED LIME ZEST,
GRUYÈRE ROLLS, AND MOLASSES-RUM
LACE WAFERS

PRAWN AND MANGE-TOUT PAELLA

THE FIRST STAGES OF COOKING—TO THE POINT OF ADDING THE tomatoes—may be done early in the day. From that point, the paella can be cooked in a 180° C/350° F/Gas 4 oven instead of on top of the stove.

780 ml/26 fl oz chicken stock
12 saffron threads, crushed
125 g/¼ lb chorizo or other spicy pork sausage, sliced into 5 mm/¼ inch rounds
4 tablespoons olive oil
1 kg/2 lb peeled and deveined large uncooked prawns
Salt
Freshly ground black pepper
175 g/6 oz mange-touts, trimmed
1 small onion, chopped
2 small spring onions (white plus some green), chopped
2 cloves garlic, finely chopped
300 g/10 oz Italian Arborio (risotto) rice or other short- or medium-grain rice
350 g/12 oz plum tomatoes, peeled, seeded and chopped
1 bay leaf
¼ teaspoon crushed dried chillies
¼ teaspoon grated lemon zest
125 ml/4 fl oz dry white wine
1 tablespoon Pernod or other anise-flavoured liqueur
4 tablespoons finely chopped fresh parsley

Pernod or any other anise spirit or liqueur has an affinity with seafood, as well as with white meat and game birds. Add it, with discretion, to the pan juices or to a seasoned butter to serve with the fish or meat.

In a large saucepan, combine the stock and saffron and bring to a simmer over medium-low heat. Remove pan from heat and cover mixture to keep it warm.

In a 35 cm/14 inch paella pan or ovenproof frying pan, cook chorizo over medium heat for about 5 minutes, or until browned. Remove from pan and drain on kitchen paper. Set aside.

Discard excess grease from pan, add 1 tablespoon of the olive oil and in it sauté prawns over medium-high heat until they just begin to turn pink, about 2 minutes. Season with salt and pepper. Using a slotted spoon, remove prawns from pan and set aside.

Add 1 tablespoon of remaining oil and mange-touts to pan and sauté over medium-high heat for about 30 seconds. Season with salt and pepper. Remove with a slotted spoon and set aside.

Add the remaining 2 tablespoons oil, the onion and spring onions to pan and cook over medium heat until softened, about 3 minutes. Add garlic and cook for about 1 minute more. Stir rice into mixture and cook, stirring until all grains are coated with oil, for about 1 minute. Stir in tomatoes, bay leaf, chilli flakes, lemon zest, wine, and 600 ml/1 pint of the warm saffron-flavoured stock and season with salt and pepper. Bring just to the boil, stirring. Reduce heat to low, cover pan and simmer for about 15 minutes, or until most of liquid is absorbed. If rice absorbs too much liquid during this time and seems dry, add remaining stock.

Discard bay leaf, sprinkle Pernod and 3 tablespoons of the parsley over rice and toss gently to distribute evenly. Arrange prawns, mange-touts and chorizo evenly over top of paella, pressing them gently into the rice, and cook over low heat, covered, for 5 to 10 minutes, or until prawns and mange-touts have finished cooking. Sprinkle with remaining parsley and serve immediately from the pan.

— 6 TO 8 SERVINGS —

BRIE AND BLUEBERRY SALAD

2	tablespoons blackcurrant vinegar
2	teaspoons fresh lemon juice
4	tablespoons hazelnut oil
4	tablespoons light vegetable oil
	Pinch grated nutmeg
	Salt
	Freshly ground pepper
1	small round (soft-leaved) lettuce, torn into pieces
1	small red-leaf lettuce, torn into pieces
2	tablespoons small fresh mint leaves
150 g/5 oz	fresh blueberries
8	thin slices (about 125 g/4 oz) brie or fresh chèvre, or goat's cheese (see Note)

In a small bowl, whisk together vinegar, lemon juice, hazelnut oil, vegetable oil and nutmeg. Season with salt and pepper and whisk until well blended.

In a large salad bowl, toss lettuces and mint leaves with just enough dressing to coat them lightly. Divide greens among 8 chilled salad plates. Scatter about 2 tablespoons blueberries over each salad, and arrange a slice of cheese in the centre of each salad. Serve immediately.

— 8 SERVINGS —

Note: If the cheese is reasonably firm, chop it into pieces the size of the berries; if very soft, put a single portion in the centre of each salad.

Ideally, salad greens should be washed and dried just before serving, but they can also be prepared earlier in the day. Rinse the leaves quickly in cold water, shake excess moisture from them and either spin them dry or pat them dry with kitchen paper or a clean tea towel. Then place each variety in a separate polythene bag, avoiding filling the bags too tightly. Refrigerate the greens until needed.

MOLASSES-RUM LACE WAFERS

A VERY PRETTY ALTERNATIVE TO ROLLING THE BISCUITS INTO CYLIN-
ders is to drape each flat, warm biscuit over the bottom of an inverted
cup or bowl, pressing to form a cup shape. The cups may be filled with
sorbet, ice cream or mousse. (For larger cups, use about 1 tablespoon of
batter for each biscuit, bake only 6 at a time, and increase the baking
time to 12 to 14 minutes.) Keep these stored in a tightly covered container and use within a few days.

```
125  g/4 oz unsalted butter
125  ml/4 fl oz (165 g/5½ oz) molasses
 90  g/3 oz light brown sugar
 70  g/2⅓ oz caster sugar
140  g/5 oz plain flour
 ¼   teaspoon ground ginger
  1  tablespoon dark rum
```

Preheat oven to 150° C/300° F/Gas 2.

In a large heavy saucepan, heat butter and molasses over low heat,
stirring, until butter is melted and mixture is smooth. Remove saucepan
from heat, add brown and caster sugars and stir until smooth. Stir in
flour and ginger, whisking briskly to remove lumps and produce a
smooth batter. Stir in rum and let batter cool slightly.

Drop teaspoonsful of batter on to a lightly greased baking sheet,
leaving at least 7.5 cm/3 inches between each biscuit (bake and work
with no more than 9 biscuits at a time). Bake in centre of oven for 10 to 12
minutes, or until biscuits have spread to about 7.5 cm/3 inches in
diameter and are bubbly.

Remove from oven and let biscuits cool for 1 minute on baking sheet.
Then, as quickly as possible, carefully lift each biscuit off with a fish
slice and roll it around a wooden spoon handle to form a neat, evenly
rolled cylinder. Place rolls on a wire rack to cool. If the last biscuits
become too hard to remove from baking sheet and roll, return them to
the oven for about 15 seconds to soften. Continue to bake and roll
biscuits in this manner until all batter is used. Store in a tightly covered
container.

— MAKES 30 TO 36 BISCUITS —

These are similar to the traditional English brandy snap. For this variation, drape the baked biscuits around a wooden spoon handle about 2 cm/¾ inch in diameter or, using a pastry horn, shape them into cornucopias. Fill the biscuits with whipped cream, using a piping bag or small spoon and allowing the cream to protrude generously at each end. Serve two per person on individual plates and offer slices of fresh juicy fruits, such as pineapple, as an accompaniment.

*L*IME ICE
WITH CANDIED LIME ZEST

SERVE THE ICE WITH MOLASSES-RUM LACE WAFERS (PAGE 227), EITHER passed separately or moulded into cups to hold scoops of the lime ice.

    The candied lime zest can be prepared up to 2 days in advance and stored in a tightly covered container until needed.

A zesting tool is useful for taking zest from limes or other citrus fruits, as the strands are stripped from the fruit easily and with no pith (which is bitter) attached.

CANDIED LIME ZEST
6	tablespoons fresh lime zest cut into julienne strips
75	g/2½ oz sugar

LIME ICE (SEE NOTE)
275	g/9 oz sugar
175	ml/6 fl oz fresh lime juice
2	tablespoons fresh lemon juice
1	size 3 egg white
4	tablespoons double cream, well chilled

Fill half a small saucepan with water and bring to the boil. Add lime zest, blanch for about 25 seconds and drain. Repeat procedure. Fill saucepan with 175 ml/6 fl oz water, stir in the sugar and bring to the boil over low heat, stirring occasionally to dissolve sugar. Stir in blanched lime zest, reduce heat to medium and simmer until liquid is syrupy and zest is glazed, about 10 minutes. Remove zest from syrup with a fork or slotted spoon and spread in a single layer on a sheet of greaseproof paper. Let cool completely.

To make lime ice, in a medium saucepan combine 500 ml/16 fl oz water with the sugar and bring to the boil over low heat, stirring occasionally to dissolve sugar. Reduce heat to medium and simmer for about 5 minutes. Remove from heat and let cool completely.

Chop candied lime zest and set 3 tablespoons of it aside for garnish. Place remaining 3 tablespoons candied zest in a large mixing bowl and stir in sugar syrup, lime juice and lemon juice. Chill in the refrigerator for at least 1 hour.

Pour chilled mixture into the container of an ice-cream maker (sorbetière) and freeze according to manufacturer's directions. About 10 minutes before ice is finished, place the egg white in a small bowl and beat with a fork until very frothy. Spoon out about 150 ml/¼ pint of the ice mixture into the bowl and blend with egg white. Add cream and blend until smooth. Pour this mixture into the ice-cream maker with remaining lime ice and finish freezing (see Note).

Place in the freezer at least 2 hours before serving. (Or store, covered, in freezer for up to 3 days before serving.) To serve, scoop balls of lime ice into individual dishes and sprinkle a generous teaspoon of reserved candied lime zest over each serving.

— 6 TO 8 SERVINGS —

Note: If you do not have an ice-cream maker, the ice can be prepared as follows: Pour prepared mixture into a shallow metal pan and place in the freezer until it becomes slushy and thick. Remove from pan and mix in a food processor, a mixer or in a bowl by hand for a few seconds. Return mixture to pan and freeze again until slushy. Repeat mixing and refreezing process. Repeat the mixing a third time, beating in frothy egg white and cream, and return mixture to pan to freeze until firm. This method will not produce as creamy an ice as a machine will, but it works very well.

AFTER THE THEATRE

MENU

◆

AUBERGINE, GARLIC AND SUN-DRIED TOMATO SPREAD

◆

LOBSTER, ASPARAGUS AND PASTA SALAD

◆

WARM FRENCH BREAD

◆

SUMMER PUDDING

OPPOSITE: AUBERGINE, GARLIC AND
SUN-DRIED TOMATO SPREAD WITH PITA,
LOBSTER, ASPARAGUS AND PASTA SALAD,
AND SUMMER PUDDING

ℒOBSTER, ASPARAGUS AND PASTA SALAD

THIS IS A VERY SPECIAL SALAD, WITH MAIN INGREDIENTS WHOSE colour, flavour, and texture complement each other beautifully. The dressing can be made a day or two ahead and stored in the refrigerator, and the salad ingredients mixed (but not dressed) several hours in advance.

1	large yellow pepper
1	clove garlic, crushed
1	sprig fresh tarragon, or a pinch dried
	Salt
250	g/8 oz thin, tender asparagus spears, trimmed
2	small live lobsters (500 to 600 g/1 to 1¼ lb)
350	g/12 oz rotelle or other spiral-shaped dried pasta

TARRAGON CREAM DRESSING

3	to 4 tablespoons tarragon white wine vinegar
1	teaspoon tarragon mustard
4	tablespoons olive oil
175	ml/6 fl oz double cream
1	tablespoon finely chopped chives
3	tablespoons chopped fresh tarragon, or 1 tablespoon dried
½	teaspoon salt
⅛	teaspoon freshly ground black pepper

TO SERVE
Fresh tarragon sprigs

Roast the yellow pepper by piercing it with a long wooden-handled kitchen fork and holding it over the flame of a gas burner until blackened and charred all over. Or grill it on a baking sheet lined with aluminium foil under a hot grill, turning it occasionally, until all sides are blackened. Drop pepper into a brown paper bag and close tightly, or wrap in aluminium foil and set aside to steam for about 20 minutes. Holding pepper under cold running water, rub off the blackened skin with your fingers. Drain the pepper and cut it in half horizontally. Remove stem, core and seeds and cut flesh into 5 mm/¼ inch strips. Set aside.

To prepare remaining salad ingredients, fill a stockpot large enough to hold the 2 lobsters with water and bring water to the boil. (Do not add lobsters at this point.) Add garlic, tarragon and 2 to 3 teaspoons salt. Tie asparagus spears together in 2 places with kitchen string and stand the bundle, tips up, in the pot. Blanch for about 2 minutes, or until just crisp-tender. Remove asparagus bundle and rinse under cold water to stop cooking. Drain, cut into 5 cm/2 inch lengths and set aside.

Bring water in stockpot back to a rolling boil and carefully lower lobsters into the pot with tongs. Cover pot until water has returned to a boil. Remove cover and cook at a rapid boil for 10 minutes. Remove lobsters from the water with tongs and drain them in a colander. Remove the smaller claw from each lobster and return claws to the pot to flavour cooking liquid. Set lobsters aside to cool.

Meanwhile, bring water back to the boil, skimming off any foam that rises to the surface. Add rotelle to the water, bring back to the boil and cook until pasta is tender but still firm, or *al dente*, about 8 minutes. Drain in a colander and rinse quickly under cold water to stop cooking. Set aside.

This salad is as versatile as it is delicious, and, should the weather turn cold, it can be made as a hot dish.

Prepare the lobster, asparagus, yellow pepper and sauce as described, but cook the pasta just before serving time. When the pasta has been drained, turn it back into the pan with 3 table-spoons olive oil and the lobster, asparagus and pepper. Warm the sauce without letting it boil. Transfer the pasta mix-ture to a heated serving dish, pour the sauce over it and serve immediately.

Crack lobster shells gently and remove meat from the tail of each in one piece, if possible. Carefully crack 2 remaining claws and try to remove claw meat intact. Set the most attractive claw meat aside to decorate pasta. Chop remaining claw meat into 2 cm/¾ inch pieces. Slice tail meat crosswise into 5 mm/¼ inch thick medallions.

In a large mixing bowl, combine lobster meat, pasta, asparagus and yellow pepper strips and toss to mix. Cover and refrigerate until just before serving.

To prepare dressing, in a small bowl whisk together vinegar and mustard and slowly whisk in oil and cream. Stir in chives, chopped tarragon, salt and pepper. Place in a covered container and refrigerate.

Just before serving time, pour dressing over salad and toss gently until well mixed. Arrange on a rimmed serving platter or in a shallow bowl. Garnish with the reserved claw meat and tarragon sprigs.

— 4 SERVINGS —

CRABTREE & EVELYN

VANILLA
Natural Flavour
- BLACK TEA -

Thé à la Vanille

25 Sachets net wt 50g 1.75 OZ

This spread also makes an excellent base for a fragrant, warming soup. Mix the full amount into 1.5 litres/2½ pints good-quality chicken stock, simmer the mixture for 10 minutes, and correct the seasoning. Serve the soup hot with 1 table-spoon grated Parmesan sprinkled over each serving if liked.

AUBERGINE, GARLIC AND SUN-DRIED TOMATO SPREAD

SUN-DRIED TOMATOES, EITHER PACKED IN OIL OR DRIED, ARE AVAIL-able in many delicatessens. The dried ones should be soaked in boiling water to cover for 15 minutes, then drained thoroughly before using.

4	cloves garlic, unpeeled
1½	tablespoons olive oil
1	medium aubergine (500 g to 750 g/1 to 1½ lb)
15	g/½ oz sun-dried tomatoes, chopped
3	tablespoons finely chopped flat-leaf parsley
2	tablespoons fresh lemon juice

¾	teaspoon sesame oil
⅛	teaspoon freshly ground black pepper
	Pinch cayenne pepper
	Salt

TO SERVE
Flat-leaf parsley
Lemon slices
Pitta bread or
savoury biscuits

Preheat oven to 200° C/400° F/Gas 6.

Brush garlic cloves with ½ tablespoon of the olive oil and wrap them all together loosely in a square of aluminium foil. Pierce skin of the aubergine in several places with a fork. Bake aubergine and garlic package on a rimmed baking tray or Swiss roll tin in centre of oven for 30 minutes; remove garlic from oven and continue baking aubergine for 40 to 50 minutes, turning it once. Remove aubergine from the oven and let cool slightly. (Both aubergine and garlic should be very soft inside.)

When cool enough to handle, squeeze garlic from the skins into a large bowl and mash with a fork to a purée. Cut aubergine in half lengthways and scoop out the soft flesh. Chop to a coarse purée and add to bowl. Add sun-dried tomatoes and parsley and toss to blend. Stir in lemon juice, sesame oil, the remaining tablespoon olive oil, black pepper and cayenne. Taste and season with salt, if necessary. Spoon spread into a serving bowl, cover and chill for at least 1 hour.

Remove spread from refrigerator well before serving to allow it to return to room temperature. Garnish bowl with parsley and lemon slices. Cut pitta bread into wedges, toast it and arrange around the bowl or on a separate plate.

— MAKES 24 TO 30 HORS D'OEUVRES —

SUMMER PUDDING

THE BRIEF MOMENT WHEN STRAWBERRIES, RASPBERRIES AND REDCUR-
rants are all ripe together is the time for the finest of summer puddings.
The only imperative for this recipe is that the bread become thoroughly
saturated with the fruit juices. The pudding should mellow in the
refrigerator for 2 days before serving.

```
250 g/8 oz raspberries
300 g/10 oz redcurrants
300 g/10 oz strawberries, sliced
100 g/3½ oz sugar
7   to 9 slices two-day-old white bread
    TO SERVE
250 ml/8 fl oz double cream or crème fraîche
```

In a large saucepan, combine raspberries, redcurrants and strawberries
with 5 tablespoons water, bring to a simmer and cook over medium-low
heat for 5 minutes, stirring once or twice. Add the sugar and stir mixture
until sugar is dissolved. Remove from the heat and let cool.

    Trim crusts from bread and line the bottom and side of a 1 litre/2 pint
pudding basin with the bread slices, cutting them to fit the basin neatly.

    Pour fruit and most of the juices into the lined basin and top with a
layer of bread cut to fit diameter of basin. Spoon remaining juice over
bread. Invert a plate small enough to fit just inside basin over top of
bread and weight it with a 1 kg/2 lb weight. Place basin on a dinner plate
and refrigerate for 2 days.

    To serve, remove weight and plate from pudding and run a knife
around the inside of the basin to loosen. Carefully invert pudding on to
a serving platter. Spoon any juices from basin or dinner plate over top of
the pudding. Serve accompanied by a jug of double cream or a bowl of
crème fraîche.

— 4 SERVINGS —

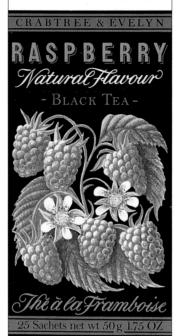

CRABTREE & EVELYN

RASPBERRY
Natural Flavour
- BLACK TEA -

Thé à la Framboise

25 Sachets net wt 50g 1.75 OZ

*This combination of
fruits can also be turned
into a popular Scandina-
vian dessert. When the
fruits have simmered for
5 minutes, purée them in
a food processor and
strain the purée. Add the
sugar, reheat the purée
until it simmers, and
then stir in 2 tablespoons
cornflour dissolved in
5 tablespoons cold water.
Bring the mixture to the
boil, stirring constantly,
just until the cloudiness
of the cornflour disap-
pears. Pour into serving
bowls, let cool and chill
until thickened. Serve
with single cream and
extra sugar.*

AS NICE AS PIE

MENU

◆

*C*HICKEN PIE WITH
LEEKS AND WILD
MUSHROOMS

◆

*O*VEN-BRAISED
TOMATOES

◆

*G*REEN SALAD WITH
WARM BACON DRESSING

◆

*H*ONEY BAKED APPLES
WITH CARDAMOM
CUSTARD SAUCE

OPPOSITE: CHICKEN PIE WITH LEEKS
AND WILD MUSHROOMS

$\mathscr{C}$HICKEN PIE WITH LEEKS
WILD MUSHROOMS

To transform an old-fashioned chicken pie into a new animal altogether, substitute a trio of fish and a simple fish stock for the chicken and chicken stock.

Buy a 250 g/8 oz piece each of cod and fresh salmon and 250 g/ 8 oz shelled raw prawns. Skin and bone the fish and cut it into 5 × 6 cm/ 2 × 2½ inch pieces.

Sauté the prawns in the butter and oil until they just turn pink, remove them with a slotted spoon and set them aside.

Dip the fish in seasoned flour and sauté it in the remaining fat until the surfaces begin to brown lightly but the fish is barely cooked. Then make up the pie in the same manner as for the chicken pie.

THIS CHICKEN AND VEGETABLE STEW CAN BE ASSEMBLED, PUT IN ITS baking dish without the shortcrust lid, and refrigerated the day before it is needed, but should be brought back to room temperature before cooking. The pastry can be made up to 2 days ahead, wrapped in cling film, and refrigerated, or made well ahead and frozen.

SHORTCRUST PASTRY
210 g/7½ oz plain flour
¼ teaspoon salt
125 g/4 oz cold lard or butter, cut into 10 pieces

CHICKEN FILLING
250 g/8 oz fresh edible wild mushrooms (see Note)
150 g/5 oz shelled fresh peas, or thawed frozen peas
75 g to 100 g/2½ to 3½ oz butter
3   tablespoons vegetable oil
2   carrots, thinly sliced
2   leeks (white and pale green parts only), washed
    and thinly sliced
750 g/1½ lb chicken thighs (about 12 pieces), boned
    and skinned
    Salt
    Freshly ground pepper
3   tablespoons plain flour
350 ml/12 fl oz chicken stock
125 ml/4 fl oz double cream
60 g/2 oz spring onions, sliced
3   tablespoons chopped fresh parsley
1½ tablespoons chopped fresh tarragon, or 1½
    teaspoons dried
1   size 3 egg yolk

To prepare pastry dough, combine flour and salt in a large mixing bowl. Add lard and toss to coat with flour. Rub lard and flour together with your fingertips until the mixture resembles coarse crumbs. Sprinkle 3 tablespoons iced water over mixture and gather into a ball. (If dough seems too dry add an additional tablespoon iced water and blend well.) Form dough into a flat disc, wrap in cling film, and refrigerate for at least 30 minutes or up to 2 days. Remove from the refrigerator 10 minutes before rolling.

Wipe mushrooms with kitchen paper to remove any dirt and slice.

If using fresh peas, place in a small saucepan of boiling water to blanch for 2 minutes; drain. Place fresh or thawed frozen peas in a 25 cm/10 inch round or square baking dish (2.5 litre/4 pint capacity).

In a large frying pan, melt 15 g/½ oz of the butter with 1 tablespoon oil. Add mushrooms and sauté over medium-high heat, stirring frequently, for about 5 minutes, until they are tender and lightly browned. Remove mushrooms with a slotted spoon and place in baking dish.

Melt 4 tablespoons of the remaining butter and the remaining oil in the same pan, add carrots and leeks, cover and cook over low heat, stirring once or twice to prevent burning, for about 10 minutes. Remove vegetables with a slotted spoon and place in baking dish.

Cut chicken into 5 cm/2 inch cubes, pat it dry with kitchen paper and season lightly with salt and pepper. Sauté in the frying pan over medium-high heat for 10 to 15 minutes, or until browned and almost cooked. Remove with a slotted spoon and add to baking dish.

About 2 tablespoons of fat should remain in the pan. (If not, add the remaining butter.) Stir flour into fat and cook over high heat, stirring constantly with a wooden spoon, for about 2 minutes. Gradually stir in the stock and cream and simmer, stirring and scraping up any brown bits, for about 5 minutes, or until sauce is smooth and thick.

Pour sauce into baking dish and stir gently to blend with other ingredients. Stir in spring onions, parsley and tarragon. Taste and season with additional pepper and salt, if necessary. (No more salt may be needed if stock made with a cube has been used, so season carefully.)

Preheat oven to 220° C/425° F/Gas 7.

On a lightly floured surface, roll pastry out to a 30 cm/12 inch round about 3 mm/⅛ inch thick. Place over baking dish and trim pastry so that only about 1 cm/½ inch extends past rim. Fold pastry under, then pinch and crimp to form a border that sits on the rim of the dish. Gather and roll out pastry scraps and cut out shapes to decorate the top of the pie, if desired. Cut several slashes in top of crust to allow steam to escape.

In a small bowl, beat egg yolk with 2 teaspoons water and brush this glaze over top and border of pie. Place pie in centre of oven, immediately reduce heat to 190° C/375° F/Gas 5 and bake for 40 to 50 minutes, or until the crust is a rich golden brown and the filling is bubbling. Serve hot.

— 6 SERVINGS —

Note: Use any combination of fresh wild or cultivated mushrooms available or reconstitute 30 g/ 1 oz dried wild mushrooms in hot water.

OVEN-BRAISED TOMATOES

USUALLY SERVED HOT, THESE CAN ALSO BE SERVED AT ROOM TEMperature, particularly with cold meats.

5	to 6 large ripe tomatoes (1 to 1.25 kg/2 to 2½ lb)
60	g/2 oz butter
1	small onion, chopped
2	whole cloves
1	tablespoon firmly packed brown sugar
¾	teaspoon salt
¼	teaspoon freshly ground pepper
4	tablespoons Crabtree & Evelyn Tomato & Chilli Sauce
1	tablespoon finely chopped fresh parsley

To make a more substantial dish, mix 90 g/3 oz fine white breadcrumbs with 60 g/2 oz melted butter and 1 teaspoon dried thyme. Sprinkle this over the onions and parsley in the dish and bake the vegetables for 30 to 40 minutes, or until the crumb topping is nicely browned.

Cut tomatoes in half and gently scoop out and discard core and seeds. Cut the flesh into quarters and set aside.

Preheat oven to 190° C/375° F/Gas 5.

In a small saucepan, melt butter over low heat. Add onion and cloves and cook over low heat for 5 minutes. Add brown sugar, salt and pepper, stirring until sugar dissolves. Add the Tomato & Chilli Sauce.

Arrange tomato quarters in a shallow, oven-to-table baking dish. Pour onion mixture evenly over tomatoes and sprinkle with parsley. Cover baking dish with aluminium foil or lid and bake in centre of oven for 20 minutes, or until tomatoes are soft but not falling apart.

Discard cloves. Serve tomatoes hot in the baking dish.

— 4 TO 6 SERVINGS —

Green Salad with Warm Bacon Dressing

WHETHER THE SALAD IS TO BE SERVED AS ONE LARGE salad or individual ones, heat the bowl or salad plates before adding the greens.

250	g/8 oz fresh spinach leaves, rinsed and torn
60	g/2 oz rocket leaves, rinsed and tough stalks removed
60	g/2 oz endive leaves, rinsed and torn
6	rashers streaky bacon
3	tablespoons vegetable oil
2	tablespoons finely chopped shallot
1	teaspoon honey
1	tablespoon coarse-grained mustard
4	tablespoons red wine vinegar
	Salt
	Freshly ground pepper
1	hard-boiled size 3 egg, finely chopped

Combine spinach, rocket and endive leaves in a large salad bowl and toss to mix.

In a large heavy frying pan, cook bacon in hot oil over medium heat until crisp, transfer to kitchen paper to drain and pour all but 4 table-spoons grease from pan. Add shallot and cook over medium-low heat until it is softened, about 2 minutes. Reduce heat to low and whisk in honey, mustard and vinegar. Season with salt and pepper.

Remove pan from heat, slowly drizzle hot dressing over greens and toss until leaves are evenly coated. Divide salad among 6 individual salad plates. Crumble a bacon slice over each serving and sprinkle each with some chopped egg.

— 6 SERVINGS —

ℋoney-baked Apples with Cardamom Custard Sauce

WARM, ROBUSTLY FLAVOURED APPLES AND A DELICATE COLD SAUCE combine beautifully in this simple dessert. The sauce would be equally delicious on stewed fruits, Madeira cake or a warm chocolate bread pudding.

CARDAMOM CUSTARD SAUCE

4	size 3 egg yolks
3	tablespoons caster sugar
500	ml/16 fl oz single cream
2	whole cardamom pods, cracked to expose seeds, or ½ teaspoon ground cardamom
½	teaspoon vanilla essence

HONEY-BAKED APPLES

6	large Golden Delicious apples
40	g/1⅓ oz currants
45	g/1½ oz stoned prunes, chopped
40	g/1⅓ oz shelled walnuts, chopped
2½	tablespoons finely chopped crystallized ginger
2	tablespoons apricot preserve
1	teaspoon grated lemon zest
¼	teaspoon ground cardamom
30	g/1 oz butter
125	g/4 oz honey
90	ml/3 fl oz orange juice
1	tablespoon fresh lemon juice
¼	teaspoon grated nutmeg

In a medium mixing bowl, beat egg yolks and sugar until pale yellow and thick.

Heat cream and cardamom pods in a medium-sized enamel or other non-reactive saucepan over low heat until small bubbles begin to form around edges. Remove from the heat and pour a small amount of hot cream into egg yolk mixture, whisking constantly. Add remaining cream, whisking. Pour mixture back into the saucepan and cook over lowest possible heat, stirring constantly, until custard thickens and coats the back of a wooden spoon, about 10 minutes. Strain through a sieve into a bowl. Add vanilla essence and stir briefly to cool. Cover the surface with cling film and refrigerate until cold.

Preheat oven to 180° C/350° F/Gas 4.

Using a small knife, core apples, keeping them whole and slightly enlarging the hollow centre. Remove peel from around one core end and about halfway down each apple.

In a small bowl, combine currants, prunes, walnuts, ginger, preserve, lemon zest and ground cardamom and stir until well blended. Stuff mixture into cored hollows of apples, packing it down firmly and mounding a small amount on top. Place apples in a well-buttered shallow baking dish just large enough to hold them.

In a small saucepan, combine butter, honey, orange juice, lemon juice and nutmeg and heat, stirring, over low heat until butter is melted and mixture is smooth. Pour over the apples and bake apples in the centre of oven, basting every 10 minutes with pan juices, for 40 to 50 minutes, or until apples are fork tender but not mushy. Remove from the oven and let cool slightly.

To serve, pour about 4 tablespoons chilled cardamom custard sauce into the bottom of each of 6 dessert dishes or shallow bowls. Place an apple in the centre of each dish and drizzle each with some of the pan juices.

— 6 SERVINGS —

As an alternative to the Cardamom Custard Sauce, beat 250 ml/ 8 fl oz double cream until it holds stiff peaks. Fold in 100 to 150 g/ 3½ to 5 oz Crabtree & Evelyn Fruit Only Blackcurrant Conserve. Its intense flavour provides a lovely balance to the sweet spiciness of the juices from the apples.

$\mathcal{B}$RIOCHE

AN IDEAL INTRODUCTION TO BRIOCHE MAKING, THIS RECIPE DOES not require the special fluted brioche tin. It is baked in a bread tin, and the recipe is simpler than the results suggest.

4	tablespoons lukewarm (40 to 45°C/105 to 115° F) water
7	g/¼ oz easy-blend dried yeast (see Note)
1	tablespoon sugar
1	teaspoon salt
350 g to 420 g/12 to 15 oz plain flour
150 g/5 oz unsalted butter, cut into pieces
4	size 3 eggs

Pour lukewarm water into a mixing bowl, stir in yeast and 1 teaspoon of the sugar and let stand for about 3 minutes, or until yeast is dissolved and mixture becomes foamy.

In a food processor, blend remaining 2 teaspoons sugar, the salt, 350 g/12 oz flour and the butter for about 15 seconds, or until the mixture resembles coarse crumbs. Add yeast mixture and process for a few seconds, or until the dough begins to form a ball. Add eggs and process for about 45 seconds, or until dough becomes smooth and sticky and begins to pull away from the side of the work bowl. If dough is too wet, add some of the remaining flour and process for a few seconds more. Scrape dough into a buttered mixing bowl, cover with a damp cloth and let rise in a warm place for 45 minutes to 1 hour, or until it is doubled in bulk.

Knock back dough and place in a buttered 21 × 11 cm/8½ × 4½ inch loaf tin. Cover with a damp cloth and let rise until doubled in bulk again, about 30 minutes.

Preheat oven to 190° C/375° F/Gas 5.

Place brioche in centre of oven and bake for 35 to 45 minutes, or until the top is deep golden brown and the loaf sounds hollow when tapped lightly on the bottom. Turn out on to a wire rack and let cool completely before slicing.

— MAKES 1 BRIOCHE LOAF —

Note: The brioche can be made with regular dried yeast, which requires about double the rising time of easy-blend yeast.

SALLY LUNN

THIS RICH YEAST BREAD RESEMBLING BRIOCHE TAKES ITS NAME, according to some, from the woman who sold it in the streets of Bath in the eighteenth century. Others claim the name derives from the French *sol-et-lune* (sun and moon), for the sunny yellow and paler tones of the crust and interior of the bread. Served warm from the oven or toasted, Sally Lunn is delicious with butter and jam.

250 ml/8 fl oz milk
125 g/4 oz unsalted butter, cut into pieces
500 to 560 g/1 to 1¼ lb plain flour
70 g/2⅓ oz sugar
1½ teaspoons salt
7 g/1¼ oz easy-blend dried yeast

3 size 3 eggs

GLAZE
1 tablespoon sugar

Sally Lunn dough may also be formed into smaller buns that are split and filled with sweetened whipped cream and sugar.

In a medium saucepan, warm milk until hot to the touch. Add butter, remove mixture from the heat and set aside, stirring occasionally, until butter is melted.

In a large mixing bowl, combine 500 g/1 lb of the flour, the sugar, salt and yeast. Pour hot milk mixture into dry ingredients and beat for about 3 minutes, or until well blended. Add eggs and beat until smooth. Add enough of the remaining flour to make a stiff batter. Cover bowl with a damp cloth and set aside to rise for 30 minutes, or until doubled in bulk.

Preheat oven to 190° C/375° F/Gas 5.

Stir down batter and spoon it into two 15 cm/6 inch soufflé dishes that have been generously buttered. Cover with a damp cloth and let dough rise for 20 minutes more, or until doubled in bulk again.

Bake in the centre of oven for 35 to 40 minutes, or until the tops are a rich golden colour and a skewer inserted in the centres of the bread comes out clean.

Meanwhile, prepare the glaze: combine the sugar and 1 tablespoon water in a small saucepan and heat over medium-low heat, stirring, until sugar is dissolved. When bread is cooked, remove from the oven and brush each loaf generously with the glaze. Return loaves to the oven for 2 minutes more to dry the glaze. Turn loaves out of the dishes on to a wire rack and let cool.

— MAKES 12 TO 16 SLICES —

GRUYÈRE ROLLS

TO GIVE THESE ROLLS A HARD, PLEASANTLY CHEWY CRUST, USE A plant mister to spray the inside of the oven with water during baking.

420 g/15 oz plain flour
7　g/¼ oz easy-blend yeast
125 g/4 oz Gruyère cheese, grated
¼　teaspoon sugar
1　teaspoon salt
300 ml/½ pint lukewarm
　　(40 to 45° C/105 to 115° F) water

In a large mixing bowl, combine 385 g/14 oz of the flour, the yeast, cheese, sugar and salt. Add the lukewarm water and stir until well blended.

Turn dough out on to a lightly floured surface and knead for about 10 minutes, adding more flour as needed to form a smooth and elastic, medium-soft dough. Or knead the dough for 5 minutes in a heavy-duty (tabletop) mixer with a dough hook.

Place dough in a buttered bowl, turning to grease all sides. Cover with a damp cloth and let rise in a warm place for about 40 minutes, or until doubled in bulk. Knock back dough.

To shape rolls, divide dough in half, then cut each half into 8 equal pieces. Working on a lightly floured surface, roll each piece of dough into a smooth ball, then elongate slightly to form an oval. Place rolls 5 cm/2 inches apart on lightly buttered baking sheets. Set them aside in a warm place and let rise for about 30 minutes, or until almost doubled in bulk.

Preheat oven to 220° C/425° F/Gas 7.

Place rolls in the centre of the oven and spray oven interior with water from a plant mister. Bake for 5 minutes and spray again. Reduce heat to 180° C/350° F/Gas 4 and bake for 15 minutes more, or until the rolls are pale golden brown and crusty. Turn them out on to a wire rack to cool.

— MAKES 16 ROLLS —

$\mathscr{S}$ALT-CRUSTED BREAD STICKS

THESE BREAD STICKS WILL STAY FRESH FOR 2 TO 3 DAYS IN A COVERED container; they also freeze well.

250	ml/8 fl oz lukewarm (40 to 45° C/105 to 115° F) water
7	g/¼ oz easy-blend dried yeast
2¼	teaspoons sugar
1½	teaspoons salt
420	g/15 oz plain flour
4	tablespoons olive oil
1	size 3 egg white
1	to 2 tablespoons coarse sea salt

Pour 4 tablespoons of the water into a small bowl, stir in yeast and ¼ teaspoon of the sugar and let stand for about 3 minutes, or until yeast is dissolved and mixture becomes foamy.

In a large mixing bowl, the bowl of an electric mixer fitted with a dough hook, or a food processor fitted with a plastic blade, combine the remaining 2 teaspoons sugar, the salt and 315 g/11¼ oz of the flour. Beat in olive oil, yeast mixture and remaining water, mixing until smooth. Gradually add enough of the remaining flour to make a moderately stiff dough. Knead until the dough is smooth and elastic—by hand, about 10 minutes; by machine, about 5 minutes. Place dough in an oiled bowl, turn it to coat it all over with oil and cover with a damp cloth. Let rise in a warm place until doubled in bulk, about 40 minutes.

Preheat oven to 170° C/325° F/Gas 3.

Knock back dough and divide into 24 equal pieces. Roll each piece of dough between the palms to make a 'rope' about 30 cm/12 inches long. (Don't worry if dough ropes are not perfectly symmetrical.) Place ropes 4 cm/1½ inches apart on two large buttered baking sheets.

In a small bowl, whisk egg white with 1 teaspoon water until well blended. Brush a little of the egg white glaze over each dough rope and sprinkle each with some of the coarse salt.

Bake bread sticks for 30 minutes, or until golden brown, dry and crisp. (If baking both sheets in the same oven, reverse positions halfway through baking so that the bread sticks brown evenly.) Let the bread sticks cool on wire racks.

— MAKES 24 BREAD STICKS —

WHOLEMEAL AND POTATO CLOVERLEAF ROLLS

THESE ROLLS HAVE THE AROMA OF A WHOLEMEAL BREAD BUT THE lightness of a traditional bread roll.

180 g/6 oz wholemeal flour
about 210 g/7½ oz plain flour
1½ teaspoons salt
1   tablespoon sugar
7   g/1¼ oz easy-blend dried yeast
1   medium potato, boiled, peeled and mashed with a
     fork
250 ml/8 fl oz milk
60   g/2 oz unsalted butter
1   size 3 egg, lightly beaten
     TO ASSEMBLE
90   g/3 oz unsalted butter, melted

In a large mixing bowl, combine the wholemeal flour with 140 g/5 oz plain flour, the salt, sugar and yeast.

In a small saucepan, heat the mashed potato with the milk and butter, stirring, until the butter is melted. Add potato mixture to the dry ingredients and stir until well blended. Whisk in the egg and add enough of the remaining plain flour to make a soft but workable dough. Turn out on to a floured surface and knead for 8 to 10 minutes, or until smooth and elastic.

Place the dough in a buttered bowl, cover and let rise in a warm place for 20 to 40 minutes, or until doubled in bulk. Knock back the dough. Lightly butter 24 bun tins. For each roll, make three 2.5 cm/1 inch balls of dough, rolling the dough between the palms of the hands. Dip each ball into the melted butter and tuck three into each tin. Let the rolls rise in a warm place for about 10 minutes, or until almost doubled in bulk.

Preheat the oven to 200° C/400° F/Gas 6.

Brush the rolls with the remaining melted butter and bake for 15 to 20 minutes, or until they sound hollow when tapped. Carefully lift each on to a wire rack to cool slightly.

— MAKES 24 ROLLS —

Cakes and breads made with mashed potatoes have a moistness, fine texture and keeping quality reminiscent of the best old-fashioned baking. The mashed potatoes are usually added hot or are mixed with part of the liquid; leftover mashed potatoes should never be added cold from the refrigerator.

*T*HE WELL-STOCKED LARDER

DIAMONDS MAY BE FINE FOR SOME, BUT A dazzling larder is the cook's best friend. Shelves brimming with herbs and spices, oils and vinegars, mustards, sauces and relishes, pastas and rices, preserved and dried fruits, sweetmeats and nuts, jams, jellies, fruit curds and honeys compose the cook's treasury.

Even the best fresh foods, carefully prepared in their prime, benefit from gentle flavouring with something from the larder. A drop of delicate wine or fruit vinegar, a spoonful of olive or nut oil, or hints of herbs or spices give a finishing touch. And, as the culinary calendar progresses from spring rhubarb to autumn pheasant, the addition of the larder's bounty from other seasons and regions produces delicious results.

Larders are as individual as their owners' kitchens and cooking. They save busy cooks time and inspired cooks time-consuming searches for ingredients. The following are some basic pantry contents and uses.

ANCHOVIES: Available as fillets packed in oil or dried salted; as a ready-made paste in a tube; and as a liquid essence in a bottle.

Pound or purée the drained fillets from a small can of anchovies into 150 g/5 oz of softened unsalted butter. Spread the anchovy butter on toast fingers to serve with soup or on toast rounds topped with slices of beef. Or gently melt the anchovy butter and serve it in a small warmed jug or sauce boat to pour over grilled meat and fish.

ANGOSTURA BITTERS: Put a few drops in light broths and vegetable soups as a final seasoning.

Add to compôtes of fresh or preserved fruit or sprinkle over grapefruit halves.

ARROWROOT

BAKING POWDER

BICARBONATE OF SODA

BISCUITS (sweet): Keep special homemade ones in the freezer; on the larder shelf store best-quality commercial butter biscuits or macaroons in sealed containers.

Extend the number of servings for a mousse or pudding by layering it with macaroons, lightly sprinkling the biscuits with flower water or a liqueur if desired.

BREADCRUMBS: Available dried, or may be made fresh and stored in the freezer.

Sprinkle over gratins and casseroles, using dried ones to absorb any butter or oil that might rise to the top during cooking (they will blend in, forming a crust) and fresh ones mixed with a little melted butter for dishes that have no other fat in them.

CAPERS: Enliven the flavour of mild, pale foods such as eggs, grilled fish, chicken fricassée and veal paprika with these salty-sharp buds.

Sprinkle over salads or add to herbed dressings.

CHESTNUTS: Available canned, either whole, dried or in an unsweetened liquid, or as a purée, sweetened or unsweetened.

CHOCOLATE: Available in plain, milk or white bars as well as chocolate chips.

FRUIT SYRUPS: On a hot day, stir 2 to 3 table-spoons fruit syrup into a glass of still or sparkling water for a delicate, refreshing drink.

GARLIC: Mash 2 to 4 peeled garlic cloves with ½ teaspoon salt and add to a mayonnaise. Eat with cold meat, steamed vegetables, salads or smoked fish.

GELATINE: Available in powdered and leaf forms.

GINGER: Keep the fresh root in the refrigerator; store ginger that is preserved in syrup or crystallized on the shelf.

Grate fresh root ginger into vinaigrettes.

Slice preserved ginger and sprinkle over peeled, sliced oranges.

HERBS: Keep dried herbs, such as bay leaf, *bouquet garni*, celery seed, mint, oregano, rosemary, sage, tarragon and thyme on the shelf; keep fresh herbs, including parsley, and herb butters in the refrigerator.

HONEY

HORSERADISH: Available bottled; buy as strong and clear-flavoured as possible.

Serve cold with roast beef, mixed with cream, liquid or whipped, for a milder flavour.

Mix with an equal quantity of grated apple, season with sugar and vinegar to taste, and serve with fish.

JAMS, JELLIES, AND PRESERVES: Fill a chocolate sandwich cake with orange marmalade.

Thin preserve slightly with brandy, kirsch, whisky, Amaretto or rum to make a filling for crêpes.

Instead of the usual apricot glaze, finish French apple tarts with a blackberry glaze.

MOLASSES

MUSHROOMS: Available dried (many varieties) for shelf storage.

MUSTARDS: Dry English; made English and French, including plain and flavoured Dijon and coarse-grained.

Mix equal quantities of honey and made mustard to make a glaze for roast ham.

Generously season a vinaigrette with Dijon mustard.

Season a béchamel sauce for cooked onions, chicory or cauliflower with 2 to 3 teaspoons of Dijon or full-flavoured coarse-grained mustard to give piquancy to the dish.

To balance the cool tastes of a Waldorf salad or coleslaw, season the dressing or mayonnaise with a honey mustard.

OATS: Store old-fashioned rolled oats.

OILS: Keep light vegetable oil, olive oil, walnut oil, hazelnut oil and oil seasoned with herbs and spices.

Sautéed foods are less likely to burn if equal amounts of oil and butter are used.

Dress a shredded carrot salad with a simple mixture of walnut oil, white-wine vinegar with herbs, salt and pepper.

Use hazelnut or walnut oils in salads of tender greens, walnuts and feta or goat's cheese.

OLIVES: Keep plain green and black, Niçoise and green stuffed with pimiento, almonds or anchovies.

PASTA: Keep the dried in the larder, the fresh in the freezer.

PEPPERCORNS: Keep black, white, green, red and mixed (with spices).

PICKLES: Store homemade or best-quality commercial dill-pickled cucumbers, gherkins and cornichons; also pickled peaches, pears and apples.

PINE NUTS: Add to stuffings for chicken, lamb and vegetables.

Gently brown in butter and sprinkle over green vegetables just before serving or over a spinach, bacon and hard-boiled egg salad.

PULSES: Available dried and canned, including lentils, white haricots, flageolets, chick-peas, kidney and pinto beans.

Dress hot, cooked lentils (or other peas or beans) with a flavourful vinaigrette, add chopped ham or bacon and serve as a warm salad.

QUAIL'S EGGS: Available bottled.

Spread a bite-size round or square of black bread with a lemony mayonnaise and top it with a slice of smoked trout and half a quail's egg.

RAISINS: Keep seeded ones for old-fashioned fruit cakes and puddings; seedless for other cooking and snacks.

Soak seedless raisins in brandy or rum for an hour and fold them into good-quality coffee or chocolate ice cream.

RICE: Stock long and short-grained white, natural brown, Italian arborio for risottos and basmati for Indian dishes.

SALT: Sea salt is best.

SAUCES: Keep a selection of homemade or commercial ones, such as Cumberland, tartare, Worcestershire and tomato (including plain ketchup).

SPICES: Keep a variety, such as allspice, caraway, cardamom, cayenne, cinnamon (sticks and ground), cloves, coriander, cumin, curry powder, ground ginger, juniper, nutmeg (whole and ground), paprika, peppercorns and dried chilli flakes.

Crush a few allspice berries into a beef stew.

Grate nutmeg over hot Brussels sprouts.

STOCK CUBES

SUGAR: Keep granulated, caster, light brown, dark brown and icing.

TOMATOES: Keep canned Italian plum tomatoes, tomato purée or paste and tomato juice, plus sun-dried tomatoes.

VANILLA: Available in liquid essence and pod forms.

VINEGAR: Store red and white wine vinegars, plain and flavoured, plus sherry, balsamic, fruit, malt and cider vinegars.

Sprinkle tarragon vinegar over hot or cold steamed green beans as a change from butter or a vinaigrette.

Sprinkle a few drops white distilled vinegar seasoned with Provençal herbs over simply sautéed or baked fish for a fresh, aromatic alternative to a squeeze of lemon.

After sautéeing fish or meat, deglaze the pan with a fruit or herbed wine vinegar to give zest to the pan juices.

Stir a few drops strawberry, raspberry or black-currant vinegar into compôtes of very ripe, sweet fruit such as strawberries, raspberries, pineapples, peaches and nectarines.

WALNUTS: Sauté the nuts lightly in butter until they are golden and fragrant; then sprinkle them over hot carrots, courgettes, or any vegetables in a béchamel sauce.

YEAST: Keep easy-blend and regular dried.